Millennium Membership

MILLENNIUM MEMBERSHIP

How to Attract and Keep Members in the New Marketplace

. . .

Mark Levin, CAE

asae

American Society of Association Executives

WASHINGTON, D.C.

Information in this book is accurate as of the time of publication and consistent with standards of good practice in the general management community. As research and practice advance, however, standards may change. For this reason, it is recommended that readers evaluate the applicability of any recommendation in light of particular situations and changing standards.

American Society of Association Executives
1575 I Street, NW
Washington, D.C. 20005
Phone: (202) 626-2723
Fax: (202) 408-9634
E-mail: books@asaenet.org

George Moffat, Vice-President
Linda Munday, Director of Book Publishing
Anna Nunan, Book Acquisitions Coordinator
Cover and interior design by Troy Scott Parker, Cimarron Design

This book is available at a special discount when ordered in bulk quantities. For information, contact the ASAE Member Service Center at (202) 371-0940. A complete catalog of titles is available on the ASAE Web site **www.asaenet.org**.

Library of Congress Cataloging-in-Publication Data

Levin, Mark.
       Millennium membership : how to attract and keep
    members in the new marketplace / by Mark Levin.
        p.   cm.
        ISBN 0-88034-163-7 (pbk.)
        1. Associations, institutions, etc.—Membership.
    2. Membership campaigns. I. Title.
    AS6 .L47 2000
    060'.68—dc21   99-050222
                                                           CIP

Printed in the United States of America.

10 9 8 7 6 5 4 3 2

To Rose
who was the first

To Morris
whose kindness knew no bounds

To Alex
who gave me laughter

To Irv
who opened so many new doors

and most of all

To Pete
who gave me everything I value

Contents

Foreword

THE POWER OF ASSOCIATION is a tremendous force in our personal and professional lives. I've always said, it's not what you know, but who you know. If I had to name the single characteristic shared by all the truly successful people I've met over a lifetime, I'd say it is the ability to create and nurture a network of contacts.

Developing networks, as I discuss in my book, *Dig Your Well Before You're Thirsty,* has never been as important. The power of networking has saved my business, my family, and my life more than a few times.

In today's shark-eat-shark economy, talent alone will not save you. Genius will not. Experience will not. Guts and hard work will not. If you need a job, money, advice, help, hope, or a means to make a sale, there's only one sure-fire place to find it—your network.

That's why I'm a huge believer in trade associations, professional societies, and chambers of commerce. These groups provide not only networking opportunities, but also valuable services, programs, and products for their members. My affiliation with the Envelope Manufacturers Association (EMA) is one of my favorite examples of the importance of making and keeping contacts. As past president of the EMA, I frequently credit my membership for a significant portion of my business success.

In *Millennium Membership,* Mark Levin shows us the new directions for membership organizations as we step into the next century. In the 35-plus years I have belonged to EMA, I have seen interpersonal contact among members enhanced by the exchange of information in electronic form. Staying ahead of trends in the industry requires more than schmoozing at a party; it may now be critical to find the right Web site to help drive sales. Mark talks about these rapid technological changes and more, while he illustrates how membership organizations will continue to be critical to success in the next century.

Mark Levin shares his insight, experience, and talent to give his readers hundreds of suggestions on how to make the power of association work for them.

> – Harvey Mackay
> Chairman and CEO, Mackay Envelope Corporation

Introduction

To BORROW A SLOGAN from the advertising world, "It's Not Your Father's (or Mother's) Organization Anymore." Attitudes about trade associations, professional societies, chambers of commerce, and other membership-based organizations have changed forever. Only the people who understand these changes—and adapt to them—will succeed in attracting and keeping members in the twenty-first century.

In fact, the challenge of membership in the next century is not only to adapt to these changes but also to make them work *for* you. That's what this book is all about.

Changing Times

A while back, I presented a membership workshop to leaders of the Medical Society of the State of New York. It was an optional program, not one required by the society during its leadership conference. The society was thrilled when nearly 200 physician and staff leaders attended the session (perhaps the snow outside the hotel had something to do with the high attendance). Startled by the turnout, we started the session by asking bluntly, "Why are so many of you here?"

The answers centered around the physicians' two greatest concerns. First was the future of their state society, which was experiencing problems with membership growth. Second, they were concerned about the future of their profession, which they realized was in even greater danger if the medical society failed to grow and maintain its position of respect and authority within the medical field.

It was heartening to see that these professionals understood how critical their society was to their profession. It was also heartening to see they were concerned enough about their society to sit through a two-hour session on membership recruitment and retention. Yes, they were leaders of their state and local medical societies, but only a small percentage were directly involved in the membership activities of those organizations. They realized that *all* leaders needed to be involved in helping the society grow; otherwise, the society was destined to continue its stagnant membership patterns.

After a spirited and open session, the attendees seemed to feel the idea of personalizing recruitment and retention efforts had real merit. Several local societies even established a short-term plan of action to recruit and retain members in a more organized fashion. Several people approached me after the program, including an older physician who said he practiced medicine in New York but was originally from Spain.

"Mark, that was a very interesting session," he stated. "I think it will help many of the local societies that are represented here today. But, you know, Mark, people really join their state and local medical societies because it is an honor and a duty."

I had to be careful how I responded to this statement. I certainly wasn't going to enter into a discussion that would seem to contradict his feelings, yet I noticed several other physicians standing nearby had overheard the comment and were awaiting my response. I decided to tell him the realities as I saw them.

"Dr. Lopez," I said, "that might be true in your country, and it might be true of your generation, but today we're facing a different challenge in a new world. The honor and duty that you felt when you joined are not necessarily there in today's, and tomorrow's, generation of physicians."

As I waited for his response, I heard another physician say, "Amen to that." Dr. Lopez said that I might have an interesting point there, one he'd think about.

New World, New Challenges

That encounter, in part, illustrates what this book is about. It's not just a case of how younger people joining organizations have a different view than the "older generation." Heck, that's been going on since the beginning of time. Things really *are* different as we head into the next millennium.

Change has always colored the way people and companies view membership organizations. In some cases, they see these organizations as agents of change. They use their organizations to help make changes in their industries, professions, or communities or in their lives. Conversely, some members see their organizations as ways to fight change, maintain the status quo, and keep some order in their business or professional lives.

Change isn't the issue that makes membership efforts in the twenty-first century challenging. What is at issue is the *speed of change.* As the pace of life quickens, people are becoming more frustrated by their inability to keep up. They expect their membership organizations to help them cope not only with what's new in their careers or businesses but also with the speed in which these new developments enter their lives. It's a daunting challenge for membership organizations, one that will grow in importance as technology continues to hasten the speed of change.

What must organizations do to meet these new challenges? Some organizations have been anticipating these changes for several years and are establishing techniques to be responsive to their members. Others are still trying to figure out what the new breed of members is looking for and how to meet those needs.

This book is for both groups. For organizations that are already changing, we hope the book will help you reach your goal of better member service more quickly. For organizations that are still struggling with the changes in the marketplace, we hope this book can help you focus your efforts to understand your members' needs and determine how to meet those needs, now and in the next century.

Six Necessary Steps

For your organization to succeed in recruiting and retaining members in the twenty-first century, you must take these six steps. (Each is covered in a separate chapter.)

1. Identify the new marketplace and learn to deal with it. This chapter pinpoints the key factors that have changed—and are changing—member expectations. It looks at what's going on in members' lives and how that affects their atttudes toward their organizations. Although most organizations can't change the things that affect the attitudes of their members and prospects, they can be prepared to acknowledge and respond to those influences.

2. Invest in technology, and use it to attract and keep members. Contrary to what some people believe, technology is not an issue; it's a given. Technology has no pros and cons—it's a part of our lives that continually changes everything we do.

The successful organization in the next century will not only acknowledge and understand the effects of technology but also use technology to attract and keep members. This chapter provides examples of how technology affects the membership decision and gives dozens of suggestions for maximizing the use of technology in membership development.

3. Move from mass marketing to mass customization. In an age when computers can maintain sophisticated data on nearly everyone and mail-merge millions of pieces of mail, too many membership organizations still use "Dear Member" as a way of communicating with their members. This chapter focuses on how organizations can—and must—use their resources to customize membership communications.

4. Maintain the human touch in the "business" of membership. Perhaps the biggest challenge to membership development is involving members in the process of helping the organization grow. More people now view membership as a staff function, and more members feel they don't have the time or the inclination to become involved in membership recruitment and retention. In this chapter, you'll find suggestions for addressing this trend.

5. Brand the organization. In the new marketplace, your organization's image will greatly influence its ability to attract and keep members. This points to the need to develop targeted, specific programs to create or enhance your organization's image among its various publics. This chapter looks at how branding has been accomplished successfully in the private sector and how membership organizations can—and must—emulate this technique.

6. Create a membership experience. This chapter shows how to tie together the other five critical elements to make membership a true experience, rather than a series of interactions or transactions. In addition to presenting a step-by-step approach to creating a membership experience, it highlights the importance of the membership team in attracting and retaining members.

Because it's difficult to remember all of the ideas presented throughout the book, we've assembled many of them in the final chapter. Refer to Chapter 7 for a list of "50 Ideas That Can Help Retain Members."

The twenty-first century holds many challenges and opportunities for membership organizations. This book can help clarify the challenges and maximize the opportunities.

CHAPTER 1

Identify the New Marketplace and Learn To Deal with It

AS YOUR ORGANIZATION MOVES into the next century, it must avoid the biggest mistake possible: trying to keep up with organizational change. Rather than keeping up with the changes in your organization, the challenge is keeping up with the changes in lives of your members. To put it simply, it's not about you. It's not about the organization. It's about the member.

To take advantage of this new marketplace, you need to understand what's going on in people's lives. You also need to understand how those factors affect members' attitudes toward their organizations. To truly understand the member and the prospective member of the future, consider the following 10 factors:

1. Technology has changed *everything*
Technology hasn't changed everything about membership organizations, but it has changed everything about people's lives. People go to work differently, communicate differently, shop differently, and think differently, all because of technology.

Key Points

Consider these 10 factors to develop an understanding of the member of the future.

1. **Technology has changed everything.**

2. **Time is the new currency.**

3. **Members and prospects measure time in many different ways.**

4. **Few memberships will be "institutionalized."**

5. **The definition of responsiveness has changed dramatically.**

6. **That which is considered unique will be valued.**

7. **Competition will increasingly come from sources other than different membership organizations.**

8. **Organizations will need to move from being service providers to being problem solvers.**

9. **Organizations will need to become more memorable to their various publics.**

10. **All effective marketing efforts take time.**

From the computer to the cellular phone to the Internet, technology has become ingrained in people's everyday lives. The question is whether your organization can connect the changes in people's lives to the ways it can help them.

Just a few years ago, a typical day in the life of an average worker consisted of doing the day's work while the "homework" piled up. Homework basically consisted of reading material—reports, periodicals, professional journals, and so forth. At the end of the day, the worker took the pile of homework and headed home. Typically, after spending time with the family or eating dinner, the worker reviewed the reading materials and created three smaller piles. One stack had been read and discarded, one included marked-up materials to be used for a future project or information, and the third pile would be given to someone else at work the next day.

That was the old marketplace.

In the new marketplace, a worker's homework consists of a laptop computer or a disk. In many cases, there isn't much to take home because the worker's home computer is already on a network with his or her computer at work. Now, the worker typically has three choices after dinner: spend time with the family, get a head start on an upcoming project, or spend time being actively involved in a membership organization. Unfortunately for membership organizations, this last option is often the lowest priority for today's workers.

Technology has created a 24-hour work day. Just glance at a person's business card in today's workplace to see what he or she—and we—are facing. On these business cards, in addition to the person's name, title, and affiliation, you'll find his or her phone number, fax number, e-mail address, pager number, car phone number, cellular phone number, home phone and fax numbers, and employer's Web site address. It's a case of "you can run but you can't hide" for most people.

Thanks to communications technology, today's workers are never out of touch with their work. Look around on a typical day and you'll see the signs of how these new communications tools have changed people's lives. You'll see cellular phones on the golf course and in supermarkets, hair salons, bowling alleys, and schools. Men and women pushing baby strollers have their ears to their phones, and even runners are seen talking as they get their daily exercise. At airports, passengers hang up pay phones to board the plane but start dialing their cell phones while walking to their seats.

However, the biggest challenge to membership organizations doesn't come from telephone technology. Instead, the biggest challenge is the Internet. Internet technology has done more than allow for 24-hour access to information, which many people used to get only from their membership organization. It also has broken down barriers between countries and time zones. People no longer worry about where information originates, because all information is instantaneous. This puts pressure on membership organizations—

even at the local and regional levels—to have a global perspective. Members have become used to getting information from anywhere and everywhere, and they expect their organizations to be able to do the same.

In addition, members can easily access information from other (often competing) organizations through Web sites. In other words, these organizations are giving your members an example of how they can meet your members' information needs.

Technology has changed people's lives to the point where, in addition to creating a new language, it is creating new meanings for old words. In the old marketplace, for example, networking was seen as a benefit of belonging to an organization. The word "networking" conveyed the image of people getting together and exchanging information and business contacts. Indeed, many membership organizations promoted networking as the reason they existed—to bring together people with similar backgrounds or interests.

Today, a visit to a major book store will reveal row after row of books devoted to networking. A close look at these networking titles tells you a lot about the new marketplace. All the books are about computers—how to build a computer network, how to network various systems, how to develop a network of your own. But no books about meeting other people.

The new marketplace is here, and it speaks to us in many ways.

Of all the trends and factors creating the new marketplace, technology is certainly the most important. (See Chapter 2 for information on using technology to your advantage.)

2. Time is the new currency

When we think of currency, money naturally comes to mind. However, the currency most people will deal in during the twenty-first century won't be dollars, rubles, pesos, or euros, which are merely units of money. Nor will it be information, a commodity that, just a few years ago, gave a huge competitive advantage to the organizations that could control its flow.

Membership organizations need to move beyond thinking that the decision to join, or to renew membership, is based on how much money membership costs. The monetary cost of membership is becoming less of an issue. Likewise, trying to convince members to join your organization because you can provide them with information has become an obsolete marketing method—anyone with Internet access can probably get more information than he or she can ever use about any possible topic.

What is the currency people deal in? *Time.* People still care about the cost of goods and services, and they still care about gathering information. But more than anything, they care about how much time it will take to get what they want.

Here's an example: For several years Brenda had been chairperson for the March of Dimes fund-raising campaign in her neighborhood. She dutifully put the names of each of the 30 families in her neighborhood on the pledge envelopes, delivered the envelopes to her neighbors, and went back to collect the contributions several days later. Last year she realized that she didn't have enough time to do the entire neighborhood, so she asked for assistance from Carol, a neighbor who had always given money to the campaign. Brenda asked Carol to collect from five houses—her own and the next four on the block.

The first words out of Carol's mouth were: "How long do you think this is going to take?"

A little stunned, Brenda replied, "It's only five houses. I've already put the names on the envelopes. Just get the donations, give the envelopes back to me, and you're done. How long can that take?"

Carol responded, "Well, you say it's only five houses. But what if they're not home? Then I'll have to go back to the ones I missed, and by then you'll be calling to see where the envelopes are, and it will just take forever. How much money are we trying to raise, anyway?"

"We're asking for $10 per household," said Brenda.

Carol quickly responded, "Why don't I just give you a check for $50, and you can divide it up among the houses?" It wasn't that Carol didn't like the March of Dimes. It wasn't the money. It wasn't that she needed more information to do the job. It was the *time.*

People today value time as much as or more than anything else they have to give. Effective membership recruiters will not only understand this fact but also make sure it's reflected in the organization's marketing efforts for attracting and keeping members.

3. Members and prospects measure time in many different ways

With so many time pressures on their personal and professional lives, people will look carefully at membership organizations to determine if those organizations are adding to or helping them cope with their time pressures. Instead of looking just at the programs, services, and products provided by the organizations, members will, in part, base their membership decisions on issues such as:

How much time will it take to get the information I want? Being able to get information isn't enough anymore. People also want to know how fast they can get it. We've entered the age when the saying "old information is useless information" has taken on new meaning. The member and prospect of the future will judge an organization partly on its ability to get information out quickly.

How much time will it take to participate in activities? For years, membership organizations have lived by this credo: You only get out of an organization what you put into it. If that's your organization's philosophy, you will have a tough time attracting and keeping members in the new marketplace. Organizations that equate the value of membership with the amount of time people spend participating are going in the opposite direction of the market. A big factor in determining whether to join—or renew—will be the amount of time necessary to participate in activities. If members believe a large amount of time is required to attend meetings and functions to get value, they may conclude that membership is not worth the investment.

How much time will it take to serve in a leadership role? This may sound like a moot point, given the fact that members are increasingly reluctant to participate in any organizational activity. However, a certain group of members, and even prospective members, will always view leadership opportunities as one benefit of membership. These people understand that leadership participation can bring many advantages above and beyond the products and services of the organization. Those advantages include greater exposure to potential customers and employers; prestige within the industry, profession, or community; access to information, individuals, and institutions that might otherwise be limited; and a chance to develop leadership skills they can use in other parts of their personal and professional lives.

Although these factors can help attract people to leadership roles, the time factor can outweigh all of them. The problem is that most people equate leadership opportunities with the "black hole" of time. They fear that, by agreeing to serve in a leadership role, they'll spend all their time in meetings and will hardly see their families or their laptop computers. This fear directly affects an organization's retention rate, because members who participate in leadership roles—anything from helping for an hour at an information booth to serving as an officer—tend to renew their memberships year after year. According to one trade association, during the 1999 renewal cycle, the overall retention rate for companies who had participated in association activities and/or had representatives serving on association boards or committees was 94 percent.

The successful membership organization in the twenty-first century must creatively structure its leadership opportunities if it is going to convince members they have enough time to be actively involved in any leadership capacity.

How much time will it take to convince my employer that membership is worthwhile? In many cases, people have to justify to a partner, a supervisor, an institution, or a spouse the money (and increasingly the time) they spend in a volunteer organization. In trade associations, as well as chambers of commerce and other corporate membership organizations, the rapid rate of corporate mergers and takeovers has had a big effect on membership. After a merger or acquisition, the association's role in the new company may change dramatically. There may be a new representative from the firm, who isn't as dedicated as the previous one. Often, the two companies involved in the merger or acquisition are both members—which means one of them will no longer be paying dues. The new company's owners or managers may not even be from the same country, so they may have a different attitude toward membership organizations than the previous managers did.

For years, professional societies and other individual membership groups have had to convince employers to support memberships. In the new millennium, this age-old challenge will be even greater. In the future the emphasis will be less on the cost of joining than on the time it will take for employees to participate. This all means additional burdens on membership organizations. First, they need to provide members with more "ammunition" to use when justifying membership to employers. Second, they need to get this information into their members' hands quickly. Members will be under increasing pressure to justify membership and to do it immediately.

4. Few memberships will be "institutionalized"

When reviewing retention rates and establishing retention strategies, many organizations focus on the 10 percent to 30 percent (or more) of members who traditionally drop out each year. These organizations believe a core group will renew each year out of loyalty to the organization or because of satisfaction with the programs and services provided.

Counting on this core group of loyal members may have been reasonable in the old marketplace, but it can cause big problems in the future because of these developments:

- Changes in ownership of companies.
- More options for members to obtain information and services.
- Increased scrutiny by corporations and institutions when evaluating annual expenditures of time and money.

This last aspect can be traced to the downsizing trend that started in the early 1990s and will continue well into the next century. Companies and institutions, either for economic reasons or because of technological advances, began cutting back on their work forces. This cutback in human resources, however, was not accompanied by cutbacks in production or lowered expectations of worker output. Companies simply learned to do more with fewer people. To maximize their reduced resources, these companies also cut costs drastically. In many instances, memberships were among the first expenses to be cut.

As these same firms became more efficient and prosperous, they didn't rejoin organizations or encourage their employees to do so. During their downsizing period, they had discovered they got along quite well without spending hundreds or thousands of dollars on memberships. What was once almost automatic—joining a trade group, paying for employees' memberships, and so forth—has become a closely watched optional expense. This puts additional burdens on membership organizations to devise an effective system to inform members of exactly what benefits they receive.

Another aspect of institutionalized membership to come under fire will be the dissolution of the programs and services that members believed they could obtain or retain only through membership. Sometimes considered "golden handcuffs" by organizations, these are programs that would ensure the continuance of membership forever because the member wouldn't want to drop out and give up that particular benefit. Programs that typically fall into this category are insurance programs, credit unions, workers compensation programs, and certification programs.

Although many of these programs will retain their value in the new century, they will no longer be the exclusive domains of membership organizations. In the bygone days of slow communications and limited choices, members often felt unqualified to compare too many insurance programs or simply didn't want the inconvenience of shopping around when their membership organization offered an alternative. In today's and tomorrow's membership marketplace, those same members will simply search for insurance options via the Internet. Instead of listening to various insurance representatives sell them a specific policy, members can simply fill out an online information form, submit it electronically to an insurance broker, and receive personalized and customized quotes quickly.

More important, the online insurance quotes will often be lower than the group policy sponsored by the membership organization. When the technology exists to scan all potential quotes in a matter of minutes and then present the best possibility, private providers have a decided advantage over many membership organizations. When a "golden handcuff" program becomes nothing more than a bidding war between the membership organization and private providers, it loses its uniqueness. As a result, the organization loses its competitive advantage.

5. The definition of responsiveness has changed dramatically

Before the advent of many of the communications techniques we now take for granted, most members were happy to receive information and services within whatever time frame the organization could accommodate. Members understood that their organizations had limited resources and couldn't be expected to drop everything whenever they called for help. After all, a limited staff can only do so much, especially in an organization having thousands of members throughout the country or the world.

Those days are over.

People are not as patient as they were just a few years ago. Again, technology is the reason. It's common knowledge that the technology for rapid response exists, and expectations have risen accordingly. To members, "quickly" used to mean as soon as the mail could be sent and received. Then quickly meant giving the information to an overnight delivery service so it could be received the next day. Next, the term became synonymous with faxing information to members. Now, quickly refers to e-mail responses and being able to download information electronically—and instantaneously.

Membership organizations have to understand that members and prospects no longer consider putting information in the mail to be a quick response to their needs. Just consider the results of a poll taken by *USA Today* to determine people's expectations of quick response. The newspaper asked people how long they would wait on hold when seeking help with a problem before getting frustrated and hanging up. Nearly 25 percent of the respondents said they would wait *less than one minute* before they hung up the telephone.

People not only expect organizations to have answers to their questions but also expect to get those answers in less than a minute. And they expect the information to be accurate. If you're not quick enough, members will move on to another organization that is more responsive. (See Chapter 2 for ways to deal with higher member expectations of quick response.) As technological advances continue, a membership organization's ability to compete in this newer, faster information-transfer field will be an important factor in a member's decision to join or rejoin.

Here's an example of how responsiveness criteria have already affected member perceptions. For many years, membership organizations have prided themselves on their publications, which were (and in may cases remain) the primary way to communicate with members. Indeed, receiving the organization's publications is considered a main benefit of membership. Organizations continue to promote their publications as the way for members to "stay up to date on the latest" in the industry or profession. Yet these publications come out annually, quarterly, or monthly. Do members and prospective members believe a magazine or newsletter that arrives every 30 days can keep them up to date when they can turn on their computers, access the Internet, and receive information in *seconds?*

Does this mean publications will no longer have value to members in the next century? Will all information be transmitted electronically? Not at all. It just calls for an adjustment in the way the value of publications is communicated to members and prospects. Information in publications needs to be valued because it is unique, useful, or enjoyable, not because it's quick.

6. That which is considered unique will be valued

To really understand the new membership marketplace, it's necessary to understand that people have more choices than ever before, about everything in their lives.

For anyone born in the United States before the mid-1960s, a synonym for the telephone company was "Ma Bell." There was only one telephone company in the country; having more than one would have been considered chaos in the business world and a source of confusion for the public. Yet less than a generation later, hundreds of telephone companies now offer an incredible range of services. The same story applies to many things people now take for granted in their lives. Back then, one or two options existed, now there are dozens and perhaps hundreds of options. Is the same true of membership organizations?

In many cases, the answer is yes. Members have more options for receiving information, networking, and receiving publications that relate to their industry or profession. With so many places to obtain products and services, why should people or companies become members? More critical is the question of why they would want to join *another* organization, because so many people and companies are already members of at least one organization. In 1996, 73 percent of all adult Americans were members of at least one nonreligious organization, according to *Giving and Volunteering in the United States,* published by INDEPENDENT SECTOR, Washington, D.C. Why pay twice for the same benefits?

To succeed in the new membership marketplace, your organization must be able to quickly and effectively differentiate itself from all the other choices members have. This requires knowing the competition and being able to point out (in a positive way) what you can offer that the competition can't. Such differentiation is becoming more difficult.

Remember, not all of the competition comes from other membership organizations. And when it does, membership marketers will be continually challenged to keep up with the new benefits offered by other groups. If you know your competition well enough, you can emphasize what your organization does that your competitors *don't do.* Too many organizations get bogged down in comparisons by saying that what they offer is better than what their competitors offer. (For instance, "Our insurance program is better than theirs" or "Only we represent you effectively in the legislature.")

Although such statements may be true, at least in the organization's view, it doesn't matter. This type of comparison merely reinforces to the member or prospect that both organizations do the same things—now it's a contest to see who does it best. If competitors offer many of the same services and programs, identify what's unique about your organization and emphasize that in membership marketing efforts.

7. Competition will increasingly come from sources other than different membership organizations

The biggest competition for membership organizations in the next century will come from other entities. This will be a new and daunting challenge for many organizations, which have primarily competed against organizations similar to themselves—not-for-profit organizations with limited financial resources. These organizations also relied heavily on volunteer input and involvement so, to some extent, the competitive "playing fields" were level.

In the millennium marketplace, the competition comes from everywhere. Competition also arises over what sources people will use to gain access to the programs, services, and benefits that they used to get exclusively from membership organizations.

Here's an example of how the real estate profession and its major membership organization, the National Association of REALTORS® (NAR), are being forced to deal with the new marketplace.

For years, many real estate professionals joined local NAR affiliates to gain access to the multiple listing service (MLS), among other services. Originally the MLS was a large book with information on homes for sale. Prospective buyers would pick out homes that interested them, and the real estate agent would take them to see the houses. For a number of years, the MLS has been a computerized, online service that often enables prospective buyers to virtually "tour" homes via the computer.

A few years ago, one of the world's largest and most successful technology firms, Microsoft, began looking at the real estate industry as a potential market for its products and services. Microsoft eventually developed a computer program to meet the needs of consumers looking for new homes. Here's an excerpt from *The Wall Street Journal* (July 13, 1998) announcing Microsoft's challenge to the MLS.

Microsoft to Open On-Line Realty Services Today

Microsoft Corp. today is launching its on-line service aimed at helping people buy homes, and the jostling with others in the real estate industry already has begun.

The software maker's new World Wide Web site, called HomeAdvisor, is aimed primarily at buyers rather than sellers and allows potential buyers to search through property listings to find houses according to criteria such as price ranges, neighborhoods, schools, and crime rates. Microsoft also is registered as a mortgage loan broker, using its site to refer people to lenders and collect origination fees.

Microsoft takes pains to position its Web site as REALTOR friendly. It directs buyers to local agents, who provide personalized services that home buyers and sellers are likely to continue to value even if they do some of their own research on-line....

"We don't feel this ever becomes an assistance-free transaction," said Larry Cohen, group product manager for HomeAdvisor. "The role of the REALTOR is here to stay."

The software company, and some rivals not affiliated with the national realtors' group, have been striking independent deals to get listing information. HomeShark Inc., based in San Francisco, and CyberHomes, based in Minneapolis, claim to have gathered as many as one million listings through such deals. They are also lobbying against the exclusive deals: in May Microsoft and competing on-line real-estate services, along with several national brokerage chains including RE/MAX International Inc., sent an open letter urging MLS boards not to enter exclusive agreements for their listings.

What's the difference between Microsoft's MLS and NAR's MLS? Not much. Eventually, both systems will probably have the same houses listed on them. So why use one system over the other?

For starters, Microsoft isn't asking anyone to join anything. Microsoft won't ask users of its system to sign a code of ethics, wear a REALTOR lapel pin, serve on any committees, or attend time-consuming meetings. It's a simple transaction: Do you want the product or not? That's all Microsoft cares about. That's also a competitive advantage.

In the article excerpt above, the Microsoft representative states that Microsoft's intent is not to take the real estate professional out of the transaction. In fact, he even says that "the role of the REALTOR is here to stay." In no part of the article, however, does he state that role of the REALTOR *association* is here to stay.

Although it is large and well funded, NAR is competing against a company with virtually unlimited resources. That's not to say the association won't remain competitive and possibly force Microsoft out of the market. It's just an example of the kind of competition membership organizations will be facing from the private sector. Private, for-profit entities with vast resources will be providing the same products and services as membership organizations and will be competing for the loyalty of the same buyers.

For many organizations, another group of competitors in the future will be *their own members*. Technology has allowed millions of people to start their own businesses and become independent suppliers and consultants to the various industries and professions in which they once were employed. The types of the services they are providing—consulting, training, and research—were previously provided by trade associations, professional societies, chambers of commerce, and other membership organizations.

This situation causes new problems for membership organizations. Not only are they facing additional competition for members and customers, but also they must determine whether special policies are needed when competing with their own members. Do you cut prices on a product or service to gain a competitive advantage, putting one of your own members out of business in the process? When soliciting bids from suppliers or awarding contracts, do you give members priority over nonmembers? What happens when your organization is considering a new product or service that is provided by a member of its governing board?

For some organizations, increased competition will come from government and quasi-government sources using the Internet and electronic data interchanges. For many years membership organizations served as a buffer between members and government entities, cutting through the proverbial "government red tape" to disseminate information to members. Now members can shortcut the process themselves by using government-sponsored Web sites and fax-on-demand services.

Quasi-governmental competition will come from sources such as other not-for-profit organizations and educational institutions. Many of these groups are becoming more aggressive in their business operations, seeking additional sources of funding. Research projects and consulting work formerly done by membership organizations are now within the marketing plans of these groups and institutions.

The Newest Competition

Perhaps the most intimidating competitor for membership organizations in the new millennium is one with a unique name. To identify this imposing competitor, take this short quiz. Look at the following list of professions and industries and guess which membership organization is *the* group in each area. (*The* group refers to the organization that represents a majority—more than half—of the practitioners within that field or industry in the United States.)

1. Physicians
A. American Medical Association
B. State and local medical societies
C. Specialty medical societies
D. None of the above

2. Association Executives
A. American Society of Association Executives
B. State and local societies
C. U.S. Chamber of Commerce
D. None of the above

3. Public School Employees
A. National Education Association
B. American Federation of Teachers
C. Independent state and local associations
D. None of the above

4. Building Contractors
A. Associated General Contractors
B. Associated Builders and Contractors
C. National Association of Home Builders
D. None of the above

5. Small Businesses
A. U.S. Chamber of Commerce
B. National Federation of Independent Business
C. State and local chambers of commerce
D. None of the above

The answer in each of these categories is D—None of the above. No organization in any of these categories represents a majority of the potential members. In some cases, the organization's membership has continued to grow but its market share (percentage of eligible members) has fallen. When the potential membership base grows faster than the organization does, what seems like progress is really a slide backward.

Possibly the most fearsome competitor in the new marketplace is "None of the above." Individuals and companies may reach the point where they believe they can get all of the benefits they seek to help their careers or business operations without joining *any* organization.

8. Organizations will need to move from being service providers to being problem solvers

To succeed in the new marketplace, membership organizations must change their overall understanding of what members and prospects want. In the old marketplace, organizations tended to measure their usefulness to members in terms of the quantity of services provided. In theory, the more "stuff" an organization could give its members, the more value they'd see in membership. With this in mind, membership organizations created as many products, services, programs, and functions as possible to maintain a competitive advantage.

According to the dictionary, the definitions of "stuff" are: 1) *unidentified materials* and 2) *worthless objects*. Why would any person or company want to join an organization that provides unspecified material and worthless objects? Members don't want, or expect, a lot of "stuff" from their organization. When asked, "What do you want in return for your dues dollars?" members most often say value.

What is value? Webster's dictionary defines value as: 1) *adequate return;* 2) *usefulness;* and 3) *worth*. People—and companies—will pay for value, or at least for perceived value. For membership organizations to continue to equate stuff with value is to ignore the changing marketplace. In the future, the definition of value won't change much, but the *perception of what provides value* will change. In fact, it already has changed.

Members and prospects are overloaded with information. Consumers, in general, are overwhelmed with choices. Membership organizations need to take advantage of this confusion and information overload by communicating with members and prospects in a more effective way.

Remember, membership is not about the organization, it's about the member (or the prospect). Organizations need to change their members' perceptions about what the organization is dedicated to doing. Is it in business to provide stuff or to help solve problems for its members? In the millennium marketplace, the answer must be: *We're here to solve problems.*

9. Organizations will need to become more memorable to their various publics

Volunteer groups traditionally have done marketing, planning, promoting, and so forth in a low-key manner. Although many groups have become more businesslike in recent years, the new marketplace calls for greater change. Facing direct competition from private entities and for-profits, membership organizations must respond by using a lot of marketing techniques borrowed from the private sector.

One marketing technique that has been used successfully in the private sector is branding. This concept is based on the idea that creating a positive image in the minds of consumers enhances the possibility of them purchasing the product. People want to feel good about what they buy. (See Chapter 5 for a detailed discussion of branding.)

10. All effective marketing efforts take time

Despite the rapid rate of change, organizations need not throw out their membership plans every time a new technology comes along or a new competitor arrives on the scene. Certainly, organizations need to keep up with changes in their members' lives and in the industry, profession, or community they serve. But that doesn't mean changing everything they do every time their markets change.

Adapting is the key, not necessarily making full-scale changes. Too many organizations have mistakenly believed their marketing efforts weren't effective because results weren't immediate. These groups need to realize that changing an organization's marketing mindset takes time.

It's always effective to be the best at what you do, to have the best programs, run the best meetings, and put out the best publications. Quality is an important factor in any marketing effort. People will pay for quality. Sticking with your plan and constantly improving and adapting your membership efforts will help attract and keep members.

On the other hand, there will be times—especially in the millennium marketplace—when being first will be as good as, or better than, being best. The ability to create a positive image can build member and customer loyalty as well as word-of-mouth sales. In some cases, an organization can literally live off of its good name for quite a while. Once the image of quality and good member service is ingrained in the minds of members and prospects, it's hard for a new organization or product to come along and quickly erase that image.

Which approach is better? A combination of the two. Start by identifying the image you want the organization to have and developing a plan to communicate that image to members and prospects. At the same time, be ready to adapt your strategies to changes in the marketplace.

Being first is good; being best is better. But being first with the best should be the goal of every organization. That doesn't happen overnight.

Invest in Technology and Use It To Attract and Keep Members

TECHNOLOGY AFFECTS EVERYTHING in the modern world. Assuming technology will continue to have this overriding influence on daily life, it makes sense to not only adapt to technology but also use technology to help recruit and retain members. Certainly, some organizations will have more money available than others to spend on upgrading technological capabilities. Even in many for-profit organizations, budget constraints determine how much can be invested in technology.

In today's marketplace, it's not uncommon for an organization to spend money on a consultant to determine its technology needs, spend more time and money obtaining proposals from various suppliers, spend time convincing the organization's leadership to budget for the systems, spend time and a lot of money upgrading old systems or installing new ones, and spend even more time and money training staff and volunteer leaders how to use the new system. Then they spend more time and money overcoming the glitches that always occur with new systems and spend time explaining to

Key Points

Technology has already changed the way members and prospects live and how they view membership organizations. In the new millennium, organizations will have to use technology effectively to attract and retain members. The starting point is to involve the membership person in the earliest stages of technological changes and systems upgrades.

Membership organizations can use technology to:

1. **Improve member and prospect tracking.**

2. **Increase the speed of response.**

3. **Improve quality.**

4. **Recognize volunteers.**

5. **Increase member involvement and interaction.**

6. **Allow for instant membership recruitment and retention.**

7. **Create new "golden handcuffs."**

8. **Use technology itself as a member benefit.**

members how to work within the new systems. At this point, one of the more technologically advanced members usually calls the headquarters office and asks why the organization is "using such an obsolete technology to serve its members."

Yes, keeping up with technology advancements can be frustrating. An organization can do only what is possible within its resources. To use technology effectively, it's essential to have a clear idea of the "big picture." Staff and volunteer leaders need to understand that the primary purpose of any new technology should be to *improve service to the members.* If this isn't the overriding rationale for any change in technology, the organization needs to reassess the proposed changes. This is why *the person responsible for the organization's membership operations should be the first to provide input into any new technological changes being made.*

This does not necessarily mean the membership person should be designing information systems or getting involved in hardware or software decisions. It doesn't mean the membership person should have any special authority to spend money or decide who the providers will be. Nor does it mean the membership person should be responsible for who has access to the new technologies once they are installed.

It does mean the membership person should provide guidance, from the earliest stages of discussion and investigation of new systems, regarding what information the system needs to gather, store, cross-reference, and disseminate. These activities, after all, are key to the membership person's success. *Does the organization's technology give the information necessary to identify the needs of members and prospects and to allow the organization to respond to those needs in a timely and empathetic manner? If not, what is the purpose of the system?*

A note of caution: Some membership organizations overlook some of their members' frustration with technology. In virtually every industry, profession, and community, you'll find a number of members and prospects who either have been overwhelmed by the speed of technological changes or have resisted them. Many of these technologically challenged members are older and do not feel e-mail, cellular phones, and the World Wide Web are necessary. They sometimes feel intimidated and disappointed if an organization to which they've belonged for a long time suddenly starts responding only to those members and prospects who can use the organization's technologies effectively.

For example, if your organization promotes its Web site as "the *only* way to stay on top of what's happening," a member without access to the Internet may wonder if the Web site has real value or is simply "high-tech stuff." Although a new generation of members believes an organization can provide real value only by making full use of available technologies, another generation of members believes they are being pushed out of the caring, comfortable organization they've always supported just because they are not technologically advanced.

Putting Technology To Best Use

Depending on how much input the membership person provides, and the level of resources available to upgrade systems, there are several ways to use technology to attract and keep members.

1. Improve member and prospect tracking

This should be the primary use of technology within a membership organization. It also should be the place that organizations with limited resources spend their money.

Before designing and investing in an organizational Web site that tells all of your publics what the organization does, spend time and money installing systems that help your organization understand what its *members* do. Gathering information about members and prospects allows your organization to do "millennium marketing." The ability to segment markets will be crucial to the success of membership recruitment and retention efforts in the next century. If your organization can't identify its market segments quickly and accurately, it will be unable to do effective mass customization—one of the six steps necessary for success.

The membership tracking system you use should be able to provide the following information on prospects:

- Basic contact information (name, address, phone, fax, e-mail, and so forth).
- Source of the name (referral from another member, attendee at a meeting or educational program, publication purchaser).
- Organizational contacts to date (membership literature sent, phone calls, direct mail solicitation, last contact made).
- Status of the prospect (a code that indicates where in the decision-making cycle the prospect is: hot prospect, new, ready for 30-day follow up).

- For individual member organizations, facts such as specialty, length of time in the profession, and title.
- For corporate membership organizations, facts such as key contact, size of company, specialty, and number of employees.
- Any information that relates to the category in which the prospect will fall.

Even with the least sophisticated membership information system, these basic facts should be storable and retrievable. If an organization can't access this type of information about its prospects, it will be difficult to recruit them.

When it comes to current members, much of the same information is needed. In addition, gather information on *any* contact the member initiates with your organization, including attendance at meetings, service in a volunteer position, purchase of publications or products, insurance program participation, and responding to a member interest survey. You may want to develop a code to represent specific information within some of these broader categories.

For example, it would be helpful to identify which publication a member purchased. This type of specific information allows you to start building a *member interest profile* as well as a member information file. The interest profile can help segment and target markets for other products, services, and programs and allow for effective cross-selling.

Perhaps the most important reason to invest in a good member tracking system is that it allows an organization to better manage its retention program. The more that is known about a member or prospect, the easier it is to customize both the recruitment and retention efforts. Having access to specific information enables you to create empathy from the earliest contact and continue that expression of empathy after the prospect joins. When your organization tracks all member contacts, the membership database becomes a unique tool in retention because it allows you to identify members who are not participating in any way. By developing a system that identifies the least active members, you're also able to identify the members who are most likely not to renew.

True, a member who doesn't participate isn't necessarily going to drop his or her membership. A certain number of members who don't participate in activities or buy products will nevertheless renew their memberships year after year. Every member has different reasons for joining and staying in an organization, which may have nothing to do with physical participation. Some members maintain memberships to support a belief or to be represented in some manner (legislatively, for example). Others want to gain recognition or stature through the affiliation or to gain or maintain something of value, such as certification.

Statistics (and common sense) indicate that members who actively participate in an organization are more likely to renew than those who don't participate. According to one trade association, during the 1999 renewal cycle, the overall retention rate for companies who had participated in association activities and/or had representatives serving on association boards or committees was 94 percent. The effective membership marketer in the twenty-first century will identify these less-active members early in the renewal cycle and target them to receive special attention, including additional mailings and phone calls. When an organization checks in with members to ensure they are receiving value from their membership, it's a sign of a caring organization—and it's bound to impress the members.

2. Increase the speed of response
If tomorrow's members and prospects won't wait one minute on the phone when seeking help with a problem, they certainly won't wait days to receive information through the postal service. Although mailings are important, membership organizations have to face the realities of modern times and

realize that many members expect them to be technologically advanced enough to use faster methods of communication.

Fax technology has become so commonplace that it's no longer considered a new technology. Just a few years ago members had to be asked if they had a fax number—now it's assumed they have one. Yet even when responding to member requests via fax, keep in mind these considerations.

Not everything is designed to be faxed. Remember that every contact with a member or prospect contributes to the organizational image being conveyed. Many print materials are designed and produced to convey color, graphics, and shading to present the best possible image. When these materials are sent through a fax machine, the graphics may become blurred, words may become unreadable, and the image of the organization may suffer.

Consider developing special or condensed versions of materials that are faxed most often, including promotional brochures, benefit statements, and applications. Format them specifically for faxing by eliminating colors and odd shadings. Work with printers or designers to produce materials that look good when faxed. Doing this addresses the need for quick response but doesn't sacrifice the quality image of your organization.

Be careful about faxing back information on a fax you have received. Not only can this be confusing, but it enables someone else (the original sender) to dictate your organization's standards of quality.

Some documents are too long to fax. Long documents tie up the receiver's fax machine and consume a lot of paper. If it is necessary to fax long documents, check with the receiver and find out if it is acceptable to send the fax after normal business hours, when it is less likely to delay or stop the transmission of other information.

Faxes can be used as an interim technology. Say a prospective member calls and asks for membership information to be mailed. Even though he or she said mail was acceptable in terms of response time, two or three days will probably pass before the information arrives. The best way to send a well-designed membership brochure is through the mail so the prospect can see the quality image conveyed by your organization. But do you want the prospect to have the impression that it always takes two or three days to receive information?

An option is to use the fax machine as an interim response method. In addition to sending the requested materials in the mail, fax a cover letter to the prospect on the same day he or she calls. Thank the prospect for his or her interest, note that the requested materials should arrive in a day or two, and include a summary of key membership benefits. The mailed materials will expand on these points and the prospect can feel free to call with any further questions. The fax and the benefits summary don't replace the mailed brochure, but such interim correspondence shows the prospect that your organization can respond promptly.

Electronic mail, commonly referred to as **e-mail,** has become the fastest growing method of rapid communication. It allows you to respond instantaneously and to communicate with others in a quick, inexpensive, and widely accepted manner. It does, however, have some drawbacks when communicating with members and prospects.

E-mail does not necessarily enhance your organization's image. As with fax technology, e-mail doesn't always allow for the transmission of the image of quality that your organization needs to project. It's important to inform employees that e-mail is not a substitute for all other means of communication with members. Common sense—and some organizational guidelines—should determine when an e-mail communication is appropriate and when to use other, more formal (although possibly slower) response vehicles.

When printed out, e-mail can resemble a ransom note. Not all e-mail remains in electronic form. Many times the receiver will print an e-mail message to have a permanent record of the correspondence. Because so many computer formats and systems exist, e-mail is rarely received in the same format in which it is sent. This changes the appearance and quality of the message on the computer screen, particularly when the message is printed. (The result often looks like a cut-and-paste message of words and phrases, a technique often used by kidnappers to create ransom notes.)

E-mail is not always confidential. Some people who are well versed in computer technology know how to intercept, read, and even alter electronic messages. These computer "hackers" present a real threat to a current or prospective member's belief that correspondence with an organization is confidential. Even within member companies, e-mail can be read by people other than the person to whom it was sent. This security issue calls for a careful determination of what information should be sent via e-mail versus other forms of communication.

E-mail should be an option chosen by members. Just because a member or prospect has the capability of communicating via e-mail doesn't mean he or she prefers that method. Many people have e-mail at their place of work but not at their home. These people (and their employers) may prefer to have communications from their membership organization handled away from the workplace. Others simply don't like using e-mail for correspondence.

Carefully review your assumptions regarding the use of e-mail. For example, not all members or prospects have access to e-mail, so it shouldn't be the only way they can receive information. Staff members may prefer communicating via e-mail because it is easier for them. In the twenty-first century membership environment, however, it's not about what's best for the organization—it's about what's best for the member or prospect. As best as you can, ascertain the person's preference for a communication method and note it in the member profile database.

Informal e-mail can look sloppy. The informality of e-mail encourages some people to use short cuts for proper grammar and punctuation. They see e-mail as a quick way to send information without having to abide by the rules of appropriate written communications. Although the proponents of e-mail insist the speed of communication is paramount, organizations need to think about the image projected by communications filled with acronyms and lacking in punctuation.

All of these considerations point to the need to establish standards for e-mail usage within your organization. The quality of the communication can directly affect the image you wish to convey.

3. Improve quality

If called upon by volunteer leaders to justify the time and expense necessary to upgrade technological capabilities, organizations should point to one reason: the ability to improve overall member service and organizational quality. This underscores the concept that organizations need to focus their resources on what helps members, not just what helps the organization.

Ways that technology can improve the quality of member service include more accurate membership records, faster response, better customization of communications and services, upgraded publications (through the use of desktop publishing software), the ability to cross-reference information, and the ability to access additional sources of information and means of communication.

4. Recognize volunteers

One area where new technology remains largely untapped is member recognition. This area should be one of the primary elements of any organization's retention program. Unfortunately, many organizations still equate member recognition with the awarding of plaques and certificates to volunteer leaders during annual meetings or recognition dinners.

Member recognition needs to be done every day. With some planning and forethought, technology can be of great use in the current and future membership environment. Take Web sites, for instance. Most organizational Web sites are designed to send information out to various publics—members, prospects, industry or professional counterparts, the general public, media, and so forth. These sites typically explain what the organization does, promote the sale of products and services, serve as a referral service or marketing vehicle for members, and supply information about the products and services that members can provide to *their* customers.

Another potential use of a Web site is member recognition, which is more than listing recent award winners or newly elected leaders (although those two groups should be accessible on the Web site). Look for reasons to list as many members as possible on your Web site in a special manner. One organization does this through an area called Heroes of the Month, which is listed on its home page along with typical areas, such as convention information, new products, and publications. Clicking on "Heroes of the Month" takes you to a list of members who have helped the organization within the past

30 days, along with their affiliation/employer, and a brief description of what they've done to earn the organization's appreciation.

The introduction to the area reads: "This month we want to thank the following people for making our organization successful." These people are not necessarily organizational leaders, and what they are being recognized for doesn't always fall into the category of a major investment of time or money. Among the listings are such activities as sponsoring a new member, assisting with fund-raising activities, hosting meetings, and speaking at functions.

This recognition page has generated positive responses. More members than ever before are accessing the organization's Web page, and many of them are checking the "heroes" section. Some may be looking for their own names, while others are curious to see if they know someone on the list. And members have been known to contact the heroes and say, "I saw your name on the organization's Web site. Congratulations." This recognition idea has created a new energy and excitement among the members, many of whom say they look forward to the updated "heroes" page each month.

Potential drawbacks to this type of recognition include the time and cost needed to update the Web site and the possibility of omitting someone who believes his or her name should be on the list. It's best to develop guidelines on whom to recognize on the Web site. Overall, however, the recognition area offers more opportunities than problems. Just the fact that a person was recognized on an organization's Web site during the year might make the difference on whether he or she renews.

You can also use e-mail to increase and speed up member recognition, assuming you have captured e-mail addresses in your membership database. When a member does something worth recognizing—even something as small as returning a survey or attending a function—send a thank you via e-mail. It's much quicker and less expensive than sending formal notes or letters and may, in some instances, be a more appropriate way of expressing thanks. The member receiving the recognition may be impressed by your organization's attention to detail and courteous show of appreciation, which can be influential at renewal time.

5. Increase member involvement and interaction

It has long been assumed that involved members won't drop out, and for the most part this has proved true. Members who are involved in their organizations tend to renew regularly and stay in the organizations longer. The trick in the millennium marketplace will be defining "involvement" in a way that attracts the new generation of members and prospects.

Traditionally, getting members involved meant having them serve in some leadership capacity—working on a committee, being an officer of a component or affiliate, and so forth. During the 1990s, it became more difficult to get members to commit to these leadership roles. If the challenge will become greater in the future, is there any hope for getting members involved and thereby raising the chances that they will renew? Certainly—*if* organizations think like their members.

In the old marketplace, the most likely way to increase involvement, besides leadership participation, was through meetings, conferences, focus groups, and educational programs. The theory: If members attend these functions and meet other members, they will more likely see the value of membership. Involvement was based on the idea, "You get out of an organization only what you put into it." The thinking was that just joining an organization and paying membership dues couldn't begin to give members the full return on their dues investment. Members had to take the next step and become involved.

The problem with using this logic now is that each of the involvement opportunity categories (leadership and activities) requires a commitment of *time*. In the new marketplace, time is the last thing members and prospects want to give. Organizations that insist on member involvement under the old definition are not listening to members, who keep saying they have little or no time.

Technology may provide one answer. A few examples of using Web sites to encourage greater involvement include:

Encouraging a greater number of (and more targeted) chat rooms, chat lines, and interactive sessions for members and prospects. This method of member interaction doesn't involve time-consuming airplane flights or cross-town automobile trips, but still offers a way for members to feel involved. In addition, members and prospects (if the chat room is open to them) can decide for themselves how much time they want to spend on this particular activity.

Perhaps just as important as the time factor is the fact that these interactions allow members to feel they can participate in a way that is *comfortable for them.* By being able to ask questions or make comments online, members can express themselves in a nonthreatening way. Some people who would never dream of standing up in a crowded room at a meeting might well raise a question or respond to a comment online.

Your organization may define involvement as participation; to members, involvement means making a connection and feeling that someone else values their input. That's why chat lines are so popular—people can see their own words added to the discussion and can receive feedback from either the host or other online participants. They know someone is listening, but they don't have to be embarrassed by walking out while someone is speaking or worry about distracting other participants by talking during discussions. It's private yet active involvement.

Many people worry that relying on Web sites and electronic give-and-take will make member involvement too impersonal and detract from the human interaction that people seek from organizations. This may be true in some cases. But organizations should also consider that online participation—in addition to empowering people who might be shy or introverted—*is also a great equalizer.* When participating in a chat room, members aren't aware of race, stature, physical limitations, economic status, or speaking ability. There are no geographic boundaries online. In some ways, the ability to be a full and equal participant is available more through electronic interchanges than in meetings and face-to-face interactions.

This does not signify a need to deemphasize meetings and physical interaction. Indeed, the networking benefit of membership is frequently an organization's competitive advantage. Web sites and chat rooms are just other options for getting members involved.

Using Web sites to seek the input of members and prospects through online surveys. Traditionally, organizations have surveyed their members and prospects through a series of member assessments—usually paper surveys mailed to members to ascertain what they wanted the organization to be doing and to rate the organization's performance in running programs and meeting member needs. These surveys were fine in the old marketplace, when members *might* take the time to respond. It's doubtful the member of tomorrow will take the time to open the envelope, pull out the survey, answer the questions thoughtfully, put the survey into another envelope, add a stamp, and then mail it back to the organization.

By enabling members to participate in online surveys, you can meet several basic needs of both the member and your organization. You'll involve more members (a retention benefit), gather valuable information (assuming the survey is well developed and credible), and do it all quickly. More members will feel involved—and they can be involved with a limited time commitment. An online survey also enables your organization to give immediate feedback; for the member to feel connected, there needs to be a "closing of the loop" in communications.

Using the Web site to allow access to the organization all the time. This might be the most obvious benefit of using technology for member involvement. Web sites give members and prospects 24-hour access to at least some of the information and resources that make membership valuable. They can access information when it's convenient for them. Even though the organization's staff and volunteer leaders aren't available all the time, its Web site is. While this access is not as good as having someone to talk to, it allows members to feel that they can get some membership involvement whenever they want it.

In the old marketplace, U.S.-based organizations faced the challenge of providing organizational assistance to members in different time zones. National organizations headquartered in the eastern United States had to project an image that all members got equal benefit, regardless of where they were located. It was, however, difficult to convince members on the West Coast of this, especially if the headquarters office closed at 5 p.m., when several hours remained in the western work day. Round-the-clock access to organizations via their Web sites not only helps overcome this problem but also provides opportunities to expand membership beyond normal geographic boundaries. Organizations that never conceived of themselves as being international can use Internet and Web site access to market their organization's benefits to people and companies everywhere.

In addition to breaking down interpersonal barriers to involvement, technology can also break down international barriers. No one cares where the organization or the member is located. What matters most is the ability to access the benefits of membership, and one of those benefits is the ability to get involved.

Organizations can also use fax technology to allow for quick and easy member involvement. Surveys via fax enable members and prospects to respond quickly, allow the organization to target specific member segments (from which they are interested in getting specific information), and permit the organization to target the least active members (the survey is one means of getting them involved).

When using fax technology (or any survey methodology), organizations need to be certain that their results are statistically valid. For example, fax and e-mail survey responses are limited to those members who have that response capability; organizations must determine if these "quick response" surveys are useful for qualitative or quantitative input.

Fax surveys also reinforce the idea that getting involved in the organization doesn't necessarily require a large time commitment. One organization emphasized this aspect by writing this message across the top of its survey: "Don't walk away from the fax machine. Please take 1 minute, fill out this survey, and fax it back right now. We *really* need your input!"

A little dramatic, perhaps, but it makes it clear to members that their participation will not take very long and that their opinions are valued. These are two important factors members consider when making the decision to renew.

6. Allow for instant membership recruitment and retention

Virtually all organizations with Web sites include areas to access information about the organization and to apply for membership. Here are suggestions for making these areas better for the member or prospect:

- Provide accurate, simple definitions of who is eligible to join in each membership category. The general public may be accessing your Web site to obtain product information or to contact a member for service. Some users also look through membership information to learn more about the organization.

- Provide an online membership application. You may need to review and revise your membership application or the membership approval procedures. If the intent of the member information section of the Web site is to encourage people to join, don't just use the Web site as an "online brochure." In other words, don't encourage prospective members to make the decision to join through an effective presentation of organizational benefits, then make them wait for an application to arrive in the mail. A complicated and involved membership application and approval process can deter membership in the new marketplace. Someone who has shown a preference for getting information and involvement in an electronic format may be discouraged by an organization that takes him or her to the brink of membership and then drags out the process.

This doesn't mean you should change your membership procedures simply to accommodate people who want quick action via the Internet. In some organizations, however, it may be worthwhile to review membership procedures. Technology's main attraction to some people is speed and convenience, and it's best not to diffuse that by relying on policies and procedures developed to meet member needs in a completely different marketplace.

7. Create new "golden handcuffs"
Membership organizations are, and will continue to be, threatened by service providers in the private sector. Traditionally, organizations viewed some of these services as something their members *had* to have—and the best, and frequently least expensive, place to get them was through the membership organization. If those days have come to an end for your organization, you'll need to create a new set of "must have" programs and services.

Technology is the catalyst for much of this competition, and membership organizations need to use it to their advantage, too. For instance, one service that may attract members is an electronic listserve, which uses e-mail messages to foster online information exchanges among members with specific interests. The key, of course, is that participants must be members to take advantage of the service. The American Society of Association Executives (ASAE), Washington, D.C., offers listserves in each of its special-interest membership sections. A message on one of these specialty group's listings noted, "This listserve alone is worth every dollar I spend to be a member. I can turn on my computer, access the list, and before our office is even open in the morning I have two or three new ideas."

Although this is only one example of the value of a listserve program, it emphasizes that the new marketplace offers opportunities to tie members to the organization in ways that are similar to the more traditional "golden handcuffs," such as insurance and group-purchasing programs. In the new marketplace, must-have programs probably will be technology based. Organizations need to find out what their members consider indispensable, then find ways to provide those services even as technologies evolve and develop.

8. Use technology itself as a member benefit

One aspect of technology that has not been applied broadly in the area of membership recruitment and retention is that the ability to access certain technologies is, in itself, a membership benefit. Organizations have an opportunity to help members and prospects cope with the new realities of their business, professional, and personal lives. Although some members may feel their organizations are forcing them to make unwanted changes in their lives, the effective and enlightened membership organization of the twenty-first century will understand and take advantage of the opportunities presented by technology.

History has shown that people will override their initial resistance to any technological advancement if it truly provides value. Inventions taken for granted today were scorned in earlier societies—the telephone, the automobile, and the airplane, to name just a few. Each of these technologies, when new, was thought by many to be a passing fad and a disruption to a more orderly world. Yet each eventually became commonplace because it provided a recognizable benefit.

There is no reason to believe that technological changes in the new marketplace will be any different. Some of the new technologies will fade, others will last longer, and some will become institutionalized in people's lives. As the widely accepted technologies gain a foothold, people will be forced to adapt to them or be left behind. Membership organizations can use this historical phenomenon to their advantage. By making members and prospects more comfortable with technologies and the accompanying advantages, organizations can prepare their members to cope better with their day-to-day challenges. The member who was afraid to jump into the potentially overwhelming world of the Internet might be reassured if his or her organization provides valuable services or information via its Web site.

There are other ways technology can be used as a member benefit. Online membership directories serve as another marketing tool for member companies and individual members who have products or services to sell. Many organizations' Web sites have links to the company or individual Web sites of their members. (This can also be a revenue producer.) Some organizations sell advertising space on their Web sites to members and nonmember companies.

Technology is a given. It will have an even greater affect on organizations, and their members, in the next century. Instead of fighting the trend, take advantage of the opportunities technology will provide in the new millennium.

Move from Mass Marketing to Mass Customization

INDUSTRIALIST HENRY FORD is generally regarded as the person who put the automobile within the reach of every American. In doing so, he changed the American way of life. Americans became mobile and adventurous, populations shifted to different parts of the country, and a feeling of equality arose among various economic classes. After all, it was reasoned, if every family could afford to have the same car—in this case, the famous Model T—then the country must be moving closer to the American dream of true equality.

Ford was able to produce the Model T at a price that everyone could afford through *mass production*. This system is based on standardizing as many aspects of production as possible to keep down the cost of producing each unit. Ford institutionalized the use of the assembly line to maintain a high rate of production. Although employees found the work repetitive, the result was a good quality product that could be sold at a reasonable price. By making all Model T cars virtually the same, Ford didn't have to retool the machinery or change production systems. Ford's concept worked so well that his company dominated the automobile industry for many years. During the height of the Model T's popularity, Ford was asked, "Can people get the car in different colors?" His legendary reply was, "Certainly. People can get the Model T in any color they want—as long as it's black." Ford's point was that making the cars in various colors would slow down production, raise production costs, and take the Model T's price tag beyond what many Americans could afford. That made no sense to Ford, who was selling millions of cars that looked alike.

Eventually, Ford's idea of the same car for all consumers ran into problems. There was (and always had been) a segment of the population that could afford something more than the basic Model T. These affluent people wanted something different than the rest of the population: cars in various colors, with more luxurious seats and interiors, and in a variety of styles. Although Ford didn't want to ignore this market, he knew he could sell many more cars to the general public compared to affluent customers. He could charge more to give the rich what they wanted, but he could also make more money by selling more cars at a lower price to the masses.

Another segment of the car-buying public that Ford overlooked was everyone who had already bought a black Model T. When they returned for a new car, their choice was still limited to a black Model T—yet they wanted something different this time. Ford had nothing else to offer, so these buyers went elsewhere, and the company's market dominance diminished.

The Rise of Personalized Service

What happened to Henry Ford had less to do with his product than with his market. Although Ford continued to produce and market a solid, stable, and low-cost product, the market for that product changed dramatically. By the time Ford realized what changes had occurred in the marketplace, he was forced to change his production methods and marketing philosophy.

Ford's experience has been relived by many membership organizations in the late twentieth century, and it will continue in the twenty-first century if those groups are not prepared to deal with the changing marketplace. Organizations have continued to "mass produce" programs, services, and benefits and market them to members repeatedly. This technique worked well for years because it was based on a simple concept: The organization has members, and all members are equal. Therefore, all members should be given equal opportunity to benefit from the organization's programs. The organization continually told members what it had to offer and let them decide which programs or services to purchase or use. In the old marketplace this technique was fine. But the millennium marketplace has moved far beyond the idea of "one size fits all."

Every day people are bombarded with customized solicitations. Technology allows companies, government agencies, and other entities to customize and personalize mailings. Direct mail that used to arrive with the greeting "Dear Occupant" or "Dear Resident" now carries the recipient's name. What's more, the body of the mailer often repeats the recipient's name several times. For the most part, the companies that send these customized solicitations have far greater resources than membership organizations. Membership organizations, however, compete directly with these private entities. The competition may not be for the same product but for the reader's limited attention and, more important, the reader's limited *time.*

Given the choice between reading a letter that begins with their name and a letter that says "Dear Fellow Member," most people will choose the personalized material. As technology continues to advance, people will have more choices from an increased number of sources. It is already possible to order a computer designed to your exact specifications, and today's automobile manufacturers offer hundreds of combinations of options. (What would Henry Ford think of *this* marketplace?) Membership organizations don't build cars or computers, but their members and potential members have become used to this customized service.

As simple as the concept of personalization and customization sounds, many membership organizations still believe they can rely on the goodwill they've established with their members and send generic communications. Yet in the highly competitive world of the millennium marketplace, any organization that takes its customers and members for granted will lose them.

Customizing Membership

In the next century, membership organizations must take steps to customize memberships within the limitations of their resources. Here are four ways to do that.

1. Develop a system that allows you to understand the different needs of various categories of members and prospects

The ability to communicate empathy to members and prospects will be critical to your success in attracting and retaining members. The competition from private, for-profit, and government sources will increase the pressure on membership organizations to use what has long been their competitive advantage: the built-in loyalty members have for their organization.

In the old marketplace this loyalty was taken for granted. In the millennium marketplace, it not only cannot be taken for granted but also must be reinforced. To do that, you have to convince members that your organization knows more about their needs than anyone else. This empathy can't come from guesswork or history. It has to come from a systematic—and frequently updated—approach to learning about members' needs.

This simple chart can be used to monitor member needs.

Type of Member/Prospect	What Do We Know About Them?	How Can We Help?

To fill in the first column, list your organization's categories of members or prospects. These categories can be as formal as the ones listed on a membership application (voting, regular, associate, and so forth) or they can be more descriptive of the work done or position held (for example, new to the profession, small business, CEO). The idea is to determine the major demographic descriptions of your membership and potential membership base. In a professional society in the healthcare field, these major breakdowns might include newly licensed practitioners, students, experienced (more than five years) in the field, working in an institutional setting, and self-employed. These descriptions would be added to the first column of the chart.

In the old marketplace, organizations jumped directly from column one (a description of the member or prospect) to column three (how can we help?). It was fine to tell the members and prospects what you had to offer people in their category and let them decide how that program or service could be of benefit. Here's how that old marketplace chart might look.

Type of Member/Prospect	What Do We Know About Them?	How Can We Help?
new to the field		reduced dues publications chapter activities
student		student chapters publications chapter activities
experienced		publications education program conventions
institutional practice		publications continuing education video library
self-employed		publications continuing education chapters

In the new marketplace, the most important column on this chart isn't the third but the second: What do we know about them? If you identify the type of member and present a list of what the organization believes would be helpful, all you've done is repackage the list of programs and activities and assign them based on the *organization's* idea of value.

The skill needed in the next century is communicating these perceived values from the perspective of the member or prospect, *not* from the organization's perspective. (Remember: It's not about you.) To do this effectively, you'll need to fill in the middle column of the chart with care. "What do we know?" doesn't mean a description of the member or prospect—that is already covered in the first column. Instead, the middle column should identify what you know about the *problems a member/prospect in this category faces every day.*

Complete the middle column entirely from the member's or prospect's perspective. Include words or phrases that describe what goes through the mind of a person in that segment when he or she goes to work each day. What are the day-to-day obstacles those members must overcome? If you can identify key elements in the second column, you'll find it easier to determine what programs, services, and values to highlight in the third column.

Using the example of a healthcare organization, here is the thought process that would help fill in the middle column of the chart.

QUESTION: What problems might someone new to the healthcare profession face?

ANSWER: Finding that first job, continuing to learn about the field, becoming economically self-sufficient, making contacts that can help him or her get started.

QUESTION: What problems might a student in the healthcare field face?

ANSWER: Lack of money (no full-time job, student loans), interest in finding a job upon graduation, balancing student life and career interests, gaining a competitive advantage in the job market.

QUESTION: What problems might an experienced (five years or longer) healthcare professional face?

ANSWER: Job security, recognition, retirement, continuing education.

QUESTION: What problems might a person working in an institutional setting face?

ANSWER: Staffing, schedules/shift work, supervisory issues, recognition, logistics.

QUESTION: What problems might a self-employed professional face?

ANSWER: Attracting new clients, business management, continuing education, taxes/finances.

By answering these questions, the organization learns not about specific programs or services (that's the organization's perspective) but about problems that need to be solved (the member/prospect's perspective). The second column, when filled in, helps determine how to communicate the value of membership. Here's how the completed chart might look.

Type of Member/Prospect	What Do We Know? (What Problems Do They Face?)	How Can We Help? (Solve the Problem)
new to the field	first job; continuing education; contacts	chapter meetings (to make contacts and learn); video library (continuing education); publications with referral services and job listings
student	no money; future job; lifestyle; competitive advantage in the job market	reduced dues; mentoring programs; student chapter activities; internships
experienced	job security; recognition; retirement; continuing education	career counseling; chapter meetings and leadership opportunities; certification; conferences
institutional practice	staffing; scheduling; logistics; recognition	special seminars; awards programs; personnel training; publications; chat rooms
self-employed	new clients; business professional; continuing education	listserves; Web site; advertising opportunities; directory listings

This chart now becomes useful for solving problems instead of simply matching membership categories and services. By focusing on helping members solve problems, an organization shifts its focus from what it does to what it can do for the member or prospect. The middle column becomes the *empathy* column. One consideration when filling in the middle column is the problem of time. Organizations should focus on their ability to help solve problems with the understanding that all of these problems are magnified by the member's or prospect's concerns about time.

Many times, staff and volunteer leaders fill in the middle column. This can be a problem if they are not in tune with the day-to-day problems of members and prospective members. Staff members may not come from the profession or business the organization represents; even if they did, they probably have been away from the field for some time. Given the rapid rate of change in the new marketplace, these staffers are unlikely to be completely up to date on changes in the workplace. As for volunteer leaders, they tend to be the more successful people in their respective fields. Although these people certainly understand the problems, they may not be in touch with the average practitioner or the new person.

The best way to fill in the middle column on this chart is to *ask current members and prospects*. It's important when talking to these members/prospects to ask the *right* questions. "What do you want the organization to do for you?" isn't the right question. Most members and prospects can't answer that. A better question would be something like, "When you get up in the morning and go to work, what are the three biggest challenges you face? What are your three biggest daily concerns?" Questions of this kind are much easier for people to answer and help to focus the information organizations are seeking.

When members and prospects answer these important questions, there is no assurance that the organization can solve all of their problems. That's not the intent of the exercise. No organization can be all things to all people. This exercise is designed to help organizations *focus their membership marketing efforts,* not develop brochures to tell members and prospects what they want to hear. Organizations shouldn't try to make promises they can't keep or offer benefits that don't exist. (On the other hand, you can use this member input to begin investigating potential new services and programs.)

2. Use membership information databases to segment and target communications efforts

Although it's important to have a sophisticated membership database, the detailed information it contains has little value if you don't use it to help customize the membership experience for members. Take advantage of the information you have gathered to segment your markets, then establish a targeted membership recruitment and retention program.

Segmenting is the technique of breaking down the total universe of members and potential members into smaller, more manageable groups. Within the membership of any organization are several smaller, more narrowly defined categories. These are not necessarily official membership categories but simply a demographic breakout that identifies a part of the total membership (or potential membership).

Depending on whether the member is an individual or a company, these segments can include such information as: how long a person or company has been a member, activities participated in during previous years, age, size of business, length of time in a profession, geographic location, and number of employees. Each organization must determine which demographic factors are most important for its needs. What's essential is having easy access to the information on those segments and the ability to use the information to customize membership recruitment and retention efforts.

Once segments of the membership and potential membership are identified and recorded, you can do targeted membership marketing. *Targeting* is the process of employing specific marketing efforts to penetrate specific segments of the market. Segmenting and targeting are the two concepts used to develop the sample membership recruitment chart. After segmenting the members and prospects into specific categories (new, student, and so forth), you can target the segments with customized messages.

Most organizations have used basic forms of segmenting and targeting for a long time. There always have been different membership brochures for different membership categories, or at least different sections of generic brochures that pointed out the benefits for various membership categories. As word processing and mail merge technologies became prevalent, organizations started producing cover letters that were segmented and targeted to various categories of potential members.

These standard techniques aren't enough in the millennium marketplace. It's necessary to move to the next levels of segmentation and targeting with virtually all communications, not just membership brochures and cover letters. In the past, for example, promoting an annual meeting or convention was simply a matter of assembling all the information into a brochure and sending the brochure to all members (and other potential attendees) repeatedly. The brochures, often beautifully designed, listed all the activities, speakers, exhibitors, and social functions. The basic premise was, "Here's what we are offering. Find something you like, and register to attend."

This type of marketing disregards two aspects of the millennium marketplace. First, it invites people to attend a meeting, a function, or an event—something that takes time. In the case of an annual meeting or convention, you're inviting them to something that takes a lot of time. And time is the one thing people have less to give than before. With the old approach, organizations are trying to convince members and prospects to give up the one thing they value more than money. (Of course, they have to give that up, too, if they want to attend the meeting.)

Second, this convention brochure is designed so the reader has to look through it to find something of interest. Members may be halfway through the brochure before they find any aspects of the meeting appealing. By that time, they may have lost interest altogether. After all, people's attention spans are so short that they will spend only a short amount of time (usually a matter of seconds, when reading a brochure or letter) before moving on to something else.

This "generic" brochure technique of marketing a meeting or conference goes back to one of the basic mistakes organizations make in dealing with the new marketplace. A generic brochure is efficient and simple for the organization—but it shouldn't be about the organization. The focus should be on the member or potential member.

In the new marketplace, you may need to use multiple brochures to attract attendees to meetings and conferences.

If six identifiable membership segments are being invited to attend, it may take six brochures to do an effective job of marketing the conference. Each brochure doesn't have to be completely different—maybe just changing the cover would suffice.

For example, brochures promoting a construction organization's annual meeting might be identical except for their covers. Each would carry a customized message, such as "Here are five reasons why a specialty contractor should attend this program" or "Here are five reasons why a general contractor should attend this program." Each highlighted list would have specific benefits for that particular market segment. In addition, the organization could develop specific marketing strategies, such as the timing of brochure mailings for each segment and color-coding the brochures to measure response rates. The key is to make sure the recipient feels the organization has a sense of what is important to him or her.

Organizations should use various methods of mass customization throughout their membership and marketing efforts. If customization is limited to the recruitment process, then members may conclude that all of the personalized, special attention was just a ploy to get them to join—that the organization doesn't really care about them as individuals. Mass customization of all membership and marketing efforts requires member information that is accurate, continually updated, and easily accessible.

3. Use all of the organization's resources to mass customize membership efforts, even in smaller organizations

Mass customization might seem overwhelming to smaller organizations that don't have the resources to create and maintain huge databases, collect and store specific information, survey members periodically, produce large quantities of customized literature, and keep track of all information. These organizations may not have staff assigned exclusively to managing information systems; in those without a full-time staff, or any staff at all, volunteers have the responsibility for membership development.

Still, small organizations can customize their membership efforts in the following ways:

- Assess your resources before tackling the customization issue. Find out if staff members or volunteers have skills in areas that would assist in customization. For instance, members who enjoy working with computers and databases might be willing to lend their talents to help create a member tracking system that could be used to customize communications efforts or to maintain the information once it's assembled.

  You may find resources among the companies that are members or among members' employers. A company might be willing to make its computer capabilities available to your organization; just be sure to consult an attorney to determine if any legal problems may arise if an outside entity has access to member records.

- Consider using volunteers or interns to develop and maintain membership information systems. If your organization has the computer capabilities but not the staff resources, ask members to volunteer to manage the information or use students to help keep records accurate. Most college and high school students are comfortable with computers and databases, and they usually are willing to work for less pay than temporary service personnel. If you're really strapped for funds, a sponsor might be willing to cover the cost of part-time help.

- Remember that collecting and storing information for customizing membership doesn't require a person to be physically located in your organization's office. This type of database work can be done anywhere, provided the person has access to appropriate computer capabilities.

- Even if your organization doesn't have the resources or desire to customize membership communications to individual members, make an effort to customize by segment or category.

Maintain the Human Touch in the "Business" of Membership

ALTHOUGH MOST MEMBERSHIP ORGANIZATIONS are not-for-profit, that designation doesn't mean they aren't businesses—they're just special types of businesses. Not-for-profit is a description given to an organization by a government agency; it is not a business philosophy. Good business practices are still essential to success, even (perhaps especially) in the case of not-for-profit organizations.

Too often, leaders of membership organizations see their challenges as being different from those faced by private, for-profit companies. In fact, you'll find more similarities than differences. This can be seen clearly when you compare the operations of a successful company to those of a membership organization.

Learning from For-Profit Businesses

As an example, consider the McDonald's Corporation, the most successful company in the fast food industry. To be successful and profitable, McDonald's has to do many things and

Key Points

As time constraints cause members to question their ability and desire to serve in volunteer leadership roles, membership organizations must guard against losing volunteer input into the membership function. Even in an era of electronic communications, membership operations require the human touch. People will still join and stay in organizations based on their relationship with other members.

Ways in which organizations can keep members involved include:

1. Identify the real barriers to member involvement.

2. Ask members to commit their talents, not just their time.

3. Communicate what members can expect to accomplish, not just what the organization expects them to do.

4. Wherever possible, break down larger membership jobs into smaller, less time-consuming tasks.

5. Use members to open doors.

6. Use members to close the sale.

do them all effectively. Summarized below are some of the functions McDonald's must perform at the highest levels to maintain its worldwide leadership in its industry. What do these have to do with voluntary, not-for-profit membership organizations? Nothing directly. However, when you compare the elements of success in business and in voluntary membership organizations, some interesting parallels emerge.

Production. A company must have a product or service to offer its customers. For McDonald's, the product is food. It has to be able to produce a broad menu of food products on a mass scale every day.

All membership organizations produce something. They just have different names for their products than private-sector firms do—terms such as programs and services. Membership organizations have a production process that includes working with suppliers, production teams, packaging, and so forth, which is similar to that used by many manufacturing or service companies. The main difference? The membership organization's overriding concern isn't making a profit on all of its products. Although membership organizations still charge for their products and services, that price doesn't always relate to a profit.

Work Force Training. McDonald's was one of the first companies in its industry to concentrate resources on providing employees with customer service training. McDonald's employees attend a specific training program to ensure they know how to prepare the products and know how to interact with customers. Although this employee training occurs at the franchise level, the parent company developed the program.

Among membership organizations with full-time employees, a critical element contributing to success is a well-trained and highly motivated staff. Training these staff members is no different than McDonald's training the workers who interact directly with its customers. The organization needs to establish an accepted way of dealing with customers (members) and communicate those standards to the work force (staff members). In the future, membership organizations will face even greater pressure to train their staffs because of the changing needs and communications capabilities of the new membership base.

Planning. To succeed in the future, a company must have an idea of where it's going, what challenges it might face, and what resources it currently has and will need, plus a set of goals for measuring success. McDonald's has established a business plan to help guide it into the future and to capitalize on the successes it has had in the past.

Almost all membership organizations have some type of strategic or long-range plan. Like its corporate counterpart, such a plan outlines the organization's goals and objectives and describes what strategies the organization will use to achieve those goals. It's really a business plan, although not-for-profit leaders often are reluctant to use terminology from the for-profit sector.

Growth/Expansion. McDonald's knows it must keep growing and expanding to remain the leader in its field. That means not only producing more products but also increasing the number of locations in which its products are sold. Each time McDonald's opens a new outlet, it increases its production capabilities. McDonald's establishes the qualifications for obtaining a franchise so it can ensure continuity and set standards that will be universally adhered to by its local managers.

A membership organization has the same challenge of finding new outlets to sell its products. The more places to buy the organization's products and services, the more chances the organization has to grow. In the nonprofit area, these outlets may be called chapters, sections, components, or affiliates. Although they have different names, these outlets basically serve the same purpose: providing locations where members (customers) can join the organization and obtain access to its products and services.

Public Relations. McDonald's has long been a leader in creating a positive image of its products and services in the minds of consumers. It has established an identity that has become almost institutionalized around the world. It has also been quick to use effective public relations techniques to respond to any crisis that arises in its operations.

Public relations aims to change the image of a product or organization in the minds of targeted publics. (See Chapter 5 for a detailed look at how membership organizations can create and communicate a desired image.) In the millennium marketplace the name of the function is irrelevant—what's important is the fact that the function is carried out.

Competing Globally. More than any other fast food company, McDonald's has aggressively pursued markets outside of its home country. The firm's reputation in the

United States has opened doors to new opportunities in other parts of the world. As is the case with many international firms, the market outside of its home country now rivals the domestic market.

Membership organizations in the next century won't be local, regional, or even national. Communications technology already has made virtually every organization international in scope. The Internet has no boundary lines, so information can—and does—come from all over the world. Just because an organization doesn't have members in other countries doesn't mean its activities lack an international aspect. Virtually all organizations will use and send information worldwide in the next century, so it's naive to think the global marketplace affects only big companies such as McDonald's.

Pricing. Despite its dominance of the fast food industry, McDonald's still faces competition in nearly all of its markets. This competition forces the company to keep up with trends in pricing and to develop pricing strategies that will keep customers interested and coming back to their stores.

Likewise, a membership organization has to charge for its products and services. The terminology is different—the basic cost of buying a membership is called "dues" instead "price"—but the idea is the same. Not-for-profit organizations can't just give away their products and services.

Product Innovation. When McDonald's introduces a new product to the public, it isn't just some idea that popped into the mind of a manager in the headquarters office. The company constantly talks to customers to find out what they like or don't like, then it test markets these products in various locations around the world. Many products never go any further than the test markets because the reaction wasn't favorable. The company makes an effort to stay in touch with customers and continually tracks changing demands. This is true not only in the food products themselves but also in the way the products are presented and the way the local outlets are operated.

Membership organizations may not consider themselves innovative, but they are constantly developing new products and services to meet the needs of their members. Although most membership organizations don't do as much test marketing as they should, almost all try to add new products based on members' input. The tool that drives product innovations in most membership organizations is the member survey. The results determine what the organization can do to help its members.

Quality Control. McDonald's, a pioneer in quality control, has long used the concept of consistent quality in food production to brand itself: Consumers could count on a certain quality of food being served in every McDonald's restaurant throughout the world. Quality control and consistency have been key to bringing customers into McDonald's.

It's somewhat difficult to compare the quality control systems that McDonald's and other producers use with quality control in membership organizations. When producing hamburgers, for example, you can identify appropriate cooking temperatures and times, develop equipment to apply a set amount of ketchup, and calibrate drink machines to dispense an exact amount into a cup. In membership organizations it's not so easy. What is the right mix of programs? Exactly what does the "right" publication look like? How do you determine when a piece of legislation is "done"? Difficult though it may be, identifying and measuring quality standards in membership organizations is a necessity in the new marketplace. In fact, the one place where membership organizations really must emulate the private sector is quality control.

In the old marketplace, members might not have gotten upset about quality lapses because they realized the limitations of membership groups. In the new marketplace, organizations will get far less consideration and be granted far fewer concessions. Members expect their organizations to establish, maintain, and exceed quality standards in virtually every area—programs, services, communications, and so on. Successful organizations will build quality standards into their strategic and business plans.

Sales and Marketing. To continue growing, McDonald's has to market its products to the consumer and market its business to potential franchise owners and investors. These marketing efforts are supported by a sales force that works with customers and suppliers to be certain that interest in McDonald's products remains high.

Just as McDonald's has a sales and marketing function, so do membership organizations. In the not-for-profit world, this area is called the membership function. Membership marketing is like any other kind of sales or marketing, except the customer is called a member. There is still a need to create as many customers as possible if the organization and its assets are to continue to grow. Without a planned program to attract and keep customers, the business or organization goes under.

Shareholder Satisfaction. As a public corporation, McDonald's has millions of owners who are constantly judging the performance of the company and their financial investments. McDonald's bases many of its marketing and management decisions on the need to provide stockholders with an acceptable return-on-investment ratio.

Membership organizations are not publicly owned companies that issue stock, so they don't have to be concerned about shareholders receiving a fair return on their investment—or do they? Again, the similarities are greater than the differences.

Membership organizations *do* have shareholders—the members. By paying dues, members become "stockholders" in the organization and in all of its programs and services. Do they expect a return on this investment of dues? Certainly.

The return can't always be expressed in dollars and cents, nor does the value of their stock go up or down with the stock market. These people, however, review their stock's performance and decide whether they want to buy the same stock again next year. In the private sector this concept is called shareholder satisfaction. In membership organizations, it's known as *membership retention*. When members renew each year, they are declaring their satisfaction with the organization's performance.

Customer Service. The bottom line in any organization is the ability to satisfy the needs of the customers. McDonald's has earned a worldwide reputation for its attention to detail and its "no questions asked" type of service. Even its marketing and branding efforts revolve around customers' needs. (For example, "You deserve a break today.")

McDonald's relies on good customer service to achieve its sales and shareholder satisfaction goals; membership organizations rely on good member service to achieve their membership and retention goals. Member service will be the cornerstone of organizational operations in the new millennium as membership groups strive to provide the best possible membership experience.

The Big Difference: Volunteers

Looking at these elements of successful business practices, it is easy to see the similarities between membership organizations and private, for-profit companies. McDonald's has succeeded by building a reputation as a big firm that still cares about each of its customers and as a company on which customers can rely for consistent quality in terms of the product (food) and the settings in their outlets. A membership organization can succeed in the twenty-first century by adopting some (or perhaps most) of the techniques that make private companies successful; regardless of its overall goals and objectives, each type of organization will be held to the same quality standards by members and customers.

The following side-by-side comparison emphasizes the similarities:

McDonald's	Membership Organizations
production	programs, services, publications
work force training	staff training
planning	strategic planning
growth/expansion	new chapters and affiliates
public relations	government/public relations
competing globally	going international
pricing	dues structures
sales and marketing	membership development
quality control	quality control
product innovation	member surveys
shareholder satisfaction	membership retention
customer service	member service

If private companies and membership organizations are similar, where do the differences arise? If the business aspects are identical, why do membership organizations require staff and volunteer leaders with unique skills to manage them? What sets membership organizations apart?

The volunteer.

Volunteer organizations are the only corporations that charge customers for their products and services and then ask the customers to help manage the company! No one has ever gone into a McDonald's and had the manager walk up and say, "I see you're enjoying that Big Mac and french fries you bought. When you're done, would you please come behind the counter and help us with our computer conversion?"

As silly as that sounds, that's exactly what happens in voluntary membership organizations. Members are charged for the products (through dues) and then are asked to participate in the management of the organization (through volunteer leadership roles). What's even more astounding is that it works—and it works well.

In the twenty-first century, a big challenge facing membership organizations is how to maintain their uniqueness. If membership organizations lose the input and involvement of volunteers, nothing will separate them from all the other producers of products and services in the marketplace. Faced with time pressures, members will have even less time to participate in their various membership organizations. Using members to sell products or recruit members is not a new concept, but it's one that needs to be nurtured in the new millennium.

Needed Adjustments

Daily, consumers all over the world are bombarded with messages from famous people telling them why they should buy a particular product, subscribe to a particular publication, or travel to a particular destination. Virtually all mass-marketed products and services today come with one of these celebrity endorsements.

It's difficult to document the first use of celebrity testimonials to sell products, but it isn't hard to imagine the dominant cave man telling his friends where he got the club he used to protect his cave and property (much as well-known law enforcement officials tell today's consumers where to buy the "club" to protect their automobiles). In medieval times, the bravest knights would recommend swordsmiths so others could purchase weapons as great as their own. Is that so different from today's athletes endorsing a line of sporting goods or recommending pain relievers that will allow others to perform their daily chores?

Everyone can name prominent people in today's society who are willing to put their name and reputation at risk by telling others to buy a particular product or service. Millions of people, through various communication channels, hear or see basketball stars telling them why to eat at McDonald's restaurants or buy Nike shoes. They receive personalized letters from television celebrities asking them to subscribe to certain magazines. They even receive computer-generated telephone calls from movie stars recommending the services of particular investment brokers and lawyers.

If these sales techniques were not effective, they wouldn't be used so frequently. For membership organizations to remain competitive with the private sector in the battle to attract and keep members/customers, they must emulate many of the successful techniques of the private sector, including the use of testimonials and endorsements.

Effective membership recruitment and retention in the new marketplace will require new attitudes, new techniques, new understanding, and new technologies. If testimonials and endorsements have been around for so long, will they still be effective in the millennium marketplace? Will anything remain the same? Will any of the "old fashioned" membership development techniques continue to be useful in the new marketplace?

Of course they will.

Many techniques that have been successful in the past still can be used in the millennium marketplace—they just need some adjustments. Instead of relying on written communications, organizations may need to use electronic communications or a combination of vehicles. Instead of asking, "What do you want us to do for you?" organizations may need to ask, "What problem can we help you solve?" Instead of providing members and prospects with a long list of programs and services in random order, organizations may need to do more segmenting and targeting of all demographic categories.

The involvement of members is one aspect of membership recruitment and retention that won't change. In membership organizations, the "celebrities" are the members. They have tried the product and are the best ones—indeed, the only ones—to endorse it.

Even in an era that will become increasingly dependent on technology to communicate the messages of values and benefits, membership organizations will need to find ways to keep their current members actively involved in helping the organization grow. In the long run, the success of every product or service will eventually depend on the testimonials given by satisfied customers.

Person to Person

The idea of involving members in membership recruitment and retention efforts may come from the old marketplace, but it will continue to be important. Here's why:

- Despite the changes occurring in communications and marketing methods, word-of-mouth marketing will still contribute to the success of any product, service, or organization. Even technology-based companies understand the necessity for satisfied customers to spread the word to others. Telephone companies offer incentives for referrals (e.g., AT&T's Friends and Family plan), while online booksellers reward customers who get others to try their products.

- In smaller organizations with limited resources, current members form the only "sales force" available. These organizations have no choice about whether to use volunteers to help them grow.

- Even in larger organizations with greater staff, financial, and technological resources, members can assist the organization in membership development.

- At a time when member involvement is taking on a new meaning, an organization's ability to get members to assist in membership growth will be a key factor in its success.

- In the new millennium, organizations must use every means possible to establish and keep an advantage over the many competitors they have for members' time, money, and loyalty. One of the few lasting advantages membership organizations have is the constant and continuing contact current members have with other members and potential members.

Adding the Human Touch

A challenge in the new millennium is persuading members to make this commitment to getting involved in the growth of their organization, especially in view of how much members' lives are changing. Although the challenge is great, it is one organizations must overcome or risk giving up the valuable and unique advantage of member involvement. Here are some suggestions on how to add the "human touch" to membership efforts.

1. Identify the real barriers to member involvement

Anticipate the concerns members will have about getting involved in membership, and show empathy in every way possible. When a member is asked to participate in the membership function—helping your organization grow in some way—he or she is likely to give one of three possible responses:

- "Sure, I'll be glad to help out."
- "I'm sorry, that's just too much time."
- "I'd be willing to help, but I wouldn't know what to do."

In the case of the first response, simply determine where to use the member in your recruitment and retention efforts. In the case of the second and third responses, however, you'll have some work to do. Note that the members didn't say they didn't like the organization or that they wouldn't recommend it to someone else. Their comments relate to themselves, not to your organization. Instead of viewing these responses as objections to participating, see them as opportunities to empathize with the member.

Many members will cite lack of time as a reason for not wanting to participate in membership activities. How will your organization empathize with members' needs to deal with time constraints and its own need to get members involved? Here are a few suggestions:

- Break down the membership jobs into smaller, less time-consuming tasks, and ask members to take on one of these.

- Find out how each member defines "too much time." Open-ended invitations to get involved in helping the organization grow will likely bring a series of rejections. The concept of an appropriate time commitment for participation will vary from one person to another. Some might think that attending a membership committee meeting three times a year is a reasonable time commitment, while others may think that giving one hour once a year to contact delinquent members is too much.

- Don't judge a member's commitment to the organization based on the number of days, hours, or even minutes he or she is willing to contribute. For instance, some members may be willing to commit a specific amount of time rather than a specific job. Whatever commitment a member makes, be prepared to use that time in a meaningful way. Be creative and flexible enough to find a role for everyone who is willing to help in any way.

In the case where a member says he or she wouldn't know what to do, begin by expressing empathy. Just because someone belongs to an organization doesn't mean he or she has the inclination or the confidence to convince others to join. To get past this response, you'll need to do two things. First, be sure the member understands that your organization would not ask someone to take on the role of recruiter without providing proper training and support. Second, remind the member that there are ways to help the organization grow besides the one-to-one recruitment of others.

In each of these cases, the key to getting members to consider taking on a job in the membership function is remembering, once again, that it's not about you. It's about the member. Expressing empathy for the member's concerns and having the member believe your organization appreciates his or her concerns is essential.

2. Ask members to commit their talents, not just their time

Concentrating on the amount of time required of a volunteer can be a big mistake. Even if your organization doesn't explicitly focus on the time commitment, the member will probably raise the point. In the new millennium, few members will come forward to commit their time simply because an organization has a preconceived notion about how many volunteers are needed and what jobs need to be filled.

Instead of focusing solely on the amount of time a member needs to spend to help the organization, identify how each member can use his or her *talents*. Through an identification of human resources, find out what skills and talents certain members possess, then match that talent pool with the work that needs to be done in various aspects of membership recruitment and retention. Focus your volunteer recruitment efforts. Say, for example, a particular member is skilled at writing. Instead of asking the member to get involved in membership activities, ask if he or she would be willing to use his or her writing skills to help the organization grow. Activities might include developing membership literature, cover letters, newsletters, magazine articles, advertising copy, and so forth. Now the member feels actively involved without focusing on how much time the effort will take.

3. Communicate what members can expect to accomplish, not just what the organization needs them to do

Another way to overcome the issue of time is to emphasize what members can expect to accomplish, not just how much time is involved. Concentrate on the important, positive outcomes of the partnership between the organization and the volunteer by pointing out what's "in it" for members who become involved in helping the organization grow. These benefits include:

• *Greater resources for the organization and the members.* Growth adds to an organization's financial and human resources. These resources can be used to create more value for members in the form of enhanced or expanded programs and services, reduced costs, and so on. All members benefit, including those who help with recruitment and retention.

• *Increased networking opportunities for members.* An important—and highly marketed—value of membership in most organizations is the opportunity to meet others from similar fields, industries, communities, or interests. Being involved with the recruitment and retention of other members gives volunteers increased exposure to these people or companies, which translates into additional business or professional contacts.

Being involved in membership is a competitive advantage for those who take the time to help recruit and retain members. In some organizations, being on the membership team is a sought-after position. (Wouldn't *all* organizations like that situation?)

• *The opportunity to develop additional personal and professional skills.* Sales, marketing, problem solving, creative thinking, delegation, and organizational management are skills that always have been valued in the work place. In many ways, successful membership recruiters are asked to use these same skills in their efforts.

The skills needed to recruit and retain members are the same as those needed to raise money for a charitable organization or to sell products and services to corporate customers. If your organization gives membership recruitment and retention volunteers the ability to develop such skills through training, literature, and discussions, the members can transfer these skills to other parts of their personal and professional lives.

4. Wherever possible, break down the larger membership jobs into smaller, less time-consuming tasks

Assume that time will always be a major factor in the minds of members when considering whether to become involved in membership, and develop a range of options for involvement. Jobs that don't require a large time commitment include:

- Using computer capabilities to assist with membership and prospect databases.
- Assisting with the development or management of the organization's Web site.
- Reviewing proposed copy for membership literature to ensure accuracy and the effective presentation of benefits.
- Submitting names of prospective members to the organization for solicitation.
- Gathering information to help qualify prospects for more effective recruitment.

5. Use members to open doors

One of the best ways for current members to feel involved in membership efforts is to introduce the membership organization to people they know or with whom they do business. Asking members to give the time needed to be an active recruiter or to serve on a membership committee is unlikely to get a positive response. Instead, ask members if they would be willing to give up 10 minutes or less to set up an appointment for an organizational representative to meet with the prospective member. Although it's preferable for a volunteer to handle the entire membership solicitation, sometimes just bringing together the organization and the prospect is an accomplishment for the member. He or she gains a personal sense of satisfaction for having assisted the organization's membership efforts in a small way. Be sure to thank the member for his or her help.

6. Use members to close the sale

This is another aspect of membership that doesn't require members to spend a lot of time. Although this part of membership work—overcoming objections and asking for money—is often the part members like least, there is a simple way to involve them. Instead of asking members to go through the entire membership recruitment presentation, ask them to share their experiences with prospective members.

In effect, the current member provides a testimonial about the value of your organization, explaining why overcoming a reluctance and joining was the best decision he or she ever made. The purpose of this brief interaction between the member and the prospect is to show another level of empathy for the prospect. The current member has credibility because he or she does the same job, works in the same environment, or believes in the same cause. The difference between a member and a staff person saying these same things is dramatic.

In a typical scenario, a staff person solicits a prospect through direct mail, telemarketing, or person-to-person meetings. The prospect may be concerned about the cost of joining or the time commitment needed to be an active member. The staff person calls a current member *who had the same concerns* when being asked to join. The current member contacts the prospect and expresses empathy for the prospect's perspective, then explains how he or she overcame such concerns; joined the organization; and found membership to be a valuable part of his or her business, professional, or personal life. The exchange between the current member and the prospect may take only a few seconds but can have a significant effect on the prospect, the member, and the organization. The prospect feels better about taking a chance by joining, the member feels involved in the membership function, and the organization gains a new member.

The Right Question

Involving members in the membership function is critical in the millennium marketplace. Membership organizations can't afford to give away their most important competitive advantage—their members. The members' credibility, belief in the organization, and desire to help the organization make for a motivated sales force.

To use this resource effectively, remember to ask the right question of current members. That's not, "Who wants to help with membership?" Rather, the right question involves identifying what talents or interests members have and determining how much time they might be willing to give to your organization. Only then can you decide how each member or group of members can help the organization grow.

Brand the Organization

THE WORD "BRANDING" may conjure up the image of a ranch hand putting his ranch's unique mark on a herd of cattle. The branding iron contacts the animals for a only few seconds, yet from then on those animals are associated with that specific ranch.

In some ways that's just what organizational branding is: identifying the organization in a unique way and creating a specific image in the minds of the targeted publics. The brand of an organization can help it stand out from other organizations, as well from the private entities with which it competes.

Branding is a relatively new concept for membership organizations but has been around for many years in the private sector. Some of the most successful branding campaigns have created images that are ingrained in the minds of consumers all over the world.

- Coca Cola: "It's the Real Thing"
- McDonald's: "You Deserve a Break Today"
- Nike: "Just Do It"

Key Points

Of the many business practices used in the private sector, branding is one that membership organizations should emulate in the new marketplace. Branding—the process of identifying an image of the organization and communicating that image to targeted groups—has seven steps.

1. **Identify your markets and what you want to say to them.**

2. **Create a visual image to complement your message.**

3. **Create "exclusivity" through name recognition.**

4. **Brand through association with a cause.**

5. **Brand through identification with quality.**

6. **Understand the challenges of creating a brand image.**

7. **Establish clear and reasonable goals for the program.**

- Exxon: "Put a Tiger in Your Tank"
- American Express: "Don't Leave Home Without It"

These may appear to be merely slogans or catchy phrases that some advertising company thought up. Certainly, the wording of a slogan or theme is part of the branding process. These slogans, however, are part of a bigger effort to create an image in the minds of the targeted public. In the case of the companies noted above, the targeted public was consumers— buyers of their products. However, researchers working with these firms found that, in addition to remembering the slogan, people associated other images with the companies. This, of course, is what the companies wanted.

In the case of Coca Cola, "The Real Thing" was a direct reference to the other cola products on the market. Coke's goal was for consumers to think of other colas as being imitation products that couldn't be as good as Coke—there can only be one "real thing."

McDonald's "You Deserve a Break Today" is one in a series of slogans that the company has used to encourage consumers to think about its restaurants as places where they can get relief from the uncertainties of life. The image of quality, the message of consistency from store to store, and the implied empathy for busy lifestyles were all part of McDonald's successful branding efforts.

It's no accident that the companies listed above have been successful and have dominated their fields for so long. Even as new competition arises, these firms have established an image that gives them a considerable advantage over newcomers. They have branded themselves in the minds of current and potential customers as being the best in their fields. Some companies have been so successful with branding that, when consumers are asked to name a company or product in their field, their firm or product is the only name that comes to mind. *That* is the ultimate in branding—when your company or product name becomes synonymous with your market (for example, Kleenex rather than tissues).

In the millennium marketplace, membership organizations need to borrow this concept of branding from the private sector. As the competition for members and prospects grows, organizations will find it harder to stand out among all the choices. Many of the competitors will be private entities with far greater resources than most membership organizations. If a membership organization can't differentiate itself from a private provider or other competitor, it will be unable to maintain membership levels. Branding techniques can help organizations move into the next century with a solid foundation on which to market their message and their membership benefits. There are seven steps to take in branding an organization to create a desired image.

Step 1: Identify Your Markets and What You Want To Say to Them

Membership organizations have numerous products or services to promote and more than one market for each, so branding can occur on several levels. Some organizations have a slogan or message to convey to their various publics. You often see these messages on organizational literature, stationery, and membership promotional materials. In many cases, these slogans are nothing more than a restatement of the obvious.

International Association of Widget Manufacturers
(organization name)
The VOICE of the Widget Manufacturing Industry
(slogan)

Of course the association is the voice of the industry— that's what all associations are supposed to be. Using this as a marketing slogan to help brand the organization is like saying, "Coca Cola—It's a Cola." In other words, it's a waste of words.

While the *theory* of branding is the same for all organizations and products, in membership organizations the *reality* is a little different. The idea is to create a positive image as well as empathy. With all the choices people have in the modern marketplace, creating empathy can truly help your organization stand out. Yet rarely do members hear a phrase or name and immediately make a connection to an organizational image.

Creating a membership marketing grid (as discussed in Chapter 3) is a good way to launch a branding effort. Take key words or phrases from the grid and explore ways to use them as core messages. Another useful exercise is to gather your staff and volunteer leaders for a brainstorming session aimed at creating an overall marketing slogan for the organization. This slogan should be succinct (short enough to put on the stationery, right under your organization's name) and should clearly articulate the image your organization desires. The slogan should also express the overriding reason your organization exists—what it stands for.

While a basic marketing slogan might be effective in creating an image among your current and potential members, it

At one of its leadership meetings, the Texas State Teachers Association (TSTA), Austin, divided staff and volunteers into small teams and asked each team to suggest a membership marketing slogan for the organization. In preparation, the participants had convened in a general session to discuss TSTA's core values, its targeted publics, and what was important to those publics.

The consensus was that TSTA represented teachers, yet there was more to the organization than that. Both staff and volunteers felt any marketing message should also express the real passion that TSTA members and employees had for enhancing the overall quality of education in Texas. After all, the participants noted, public education is as much about the students as about the teachers, so there needs to be a link between who TSTA represents and who its *members* represent.

After a lengthy session of idea sharing, one slogan seemed to get to the heart of the matter more than others: *TSTA—You Take Care of the Students, We Take Care of You.* This slogan not only created an image but also created *empathy.* Any teacher can hear that slogan and think, "Well, at least that organization knows who we are and what we do for a living." Although TSTA did not adopt this phrase as its official slogan, the exercise helped association leaders refocus their marketing efforts.

wouldn't necessarily mean anything to other targeted audiences, such as political leaders or the general public. For those groups, you might need to come up with a different slogan.

The same is true with your product lines. Some organizations create a marketing slogan for their educational programs, conferences, publications, Web sites, and so forth. In addition to different slogans for different product lines, some organizations even develop different slogans for different market segments for each of their product lines. Of course, it's not necessary to go to those lengths unless your organization has the resources to do so.

Step 2: Create a Visual Image To Complement Your Message

Along with a slogan or verbal message, organizations can brand themselves through visual images. Again, the private sector has been a leader in this area. Think of the golden arches that have become synonymous with McDonald's, the "swoosh" logo associated with Nike shoes, and the ticking stopwatch that signals the television program 60 Minutes—all are examples of visual brand images.

Although a membership organization can use this visual branding technique, too, proceed with caution. You're not just selling a product or service, so your visual symbols and slogans need to be in keeping with your organization's culture. When implementing a branding campaign, you don't necessarily need to retire a logo that has been used by the organization since its inception, although a new logo will frequently encourage people to take note of the communication or message.

If your organization wants to keep its traditional logo and still change its image, attach a branding slogan to the logo. Simply putting the marketing slogan under the logo can link the images in the minds of your targeted publics. Or when your organization changes and updates its logo, take advantage of the opportunity to add a new marketing slogan. The new images will not only attract new members and interest but they also will generate enthusiasm among current members.

One successful campaign to upgrade and change images in the commodity field used the slogan "Got Milk?" The milk producers (the National Fluid Milk Processor Promotion Board) linked the slogan with images of famous sports and entertainment personalities who had milk "mustaches." The milk industry ran the ads thousands of times in various media venues until the two images became one in the public's mind: It was almost impossible to see a celebrity with a white mustache and not think of the words "Got milk?" The industry has successfully linked the images and branded them in the minds of consumers, its targeted market.

Among membership organizations, the American Institute of Certified Public Accountants (AICPA), New York, N.Y., set about changing the public's image of its members and emphasizing the value its members bring to their employers. Through surveys and research, AICPA knew most people thought of accountants in the traditional sense, as auditors, bookkeepers, detail-oriented statisticians, and tax preparers. While AICPA certainly didn't want people to think its members couldn't do all of these things, it did want to broaden the public's image about what else its members could do.

AICPA embarked on a major effort to change the image of its members among its various publics, which included producing and distributing messages through a variety of media (videos, printed materials, and television spots). Focusing on the idea that its members could be effective problem solvers, the organization created images of CPAs performing a wide range of valuable functions within the business community and within society at large. These included keeping businesses out of trouble, providing factual insight into company problems, and being an important part of the planning process. All of these images related to the targeted public (the business community), not to AICPA or its members. AICPA's affiliated organizations throughout the United States supplemented these national efforts by customizing the materials and messages to be relevant to local issues.

In addition to creating a new image of its members' value, AICPA branded the campaign further by using a slogan with each message. The slogans—such as "The CPA. Never Underestimate the Value"—reinforced the image that CPAs provide a wide range of services and are not limited to traditional roles. AICPA is using both messages and images to brand the concept of value into the minds of its publics and to associate its members (who are identifiable by that brand) as part of the value.

Step 3: Create "Exclusivity" Through Name Recognition

Consistency and repetition are two important components of the branding process. Whatever the message or image your organization wants to project, keep it in front of your targeted publics as frequently as possible. Mixed messages can result in mixed images, so keep your image recognizable and consistent.

Once your organization has selected a symbol or logo, use it everywhere: on letterhead, brochures, advertising copy, invoices, renewal notices, fax forms, and Web sites (each page). Through repeated exposure to the logo and slogan, people will begin to associate your organization with the image the slogans and logos are designed to create. Eventually, if the brand message is strong enough, the targeted publics will begin building trust in your organization. Take advantage of this trust to communicate other messages. For example, if your organization has established its credibility as being the only (or primary) source of information in a particular area, use that influence to market products and services as well as memberships.

This repeated use of your organization's brand is aimed at creating an image of exclusivity. In other words, people and companies not only come to associate an organization with its image, they associate *only* that organization with that image. There's no confusion about which organization or product is affiliated with the brand, which is why branding is a *competitive advantage*.

Step 4: Brand Through Association with a Cause

In the millennium marketplace, the increased competition to provide information and products may limit the ability of membership organizations to convince people they can deliver these products better, faster, or cheaper than private providers. One way to overcome this reliance on products is to create a branding strategy that associates your organization with a cause. This type of branding provides several opportunities. It:

- Creates an emotional attachment to the organization.
- Brands the organization as a caring organization.
- Provides additional adrenaline to the organization.
- Provides additional focus for the organization.
- Gives members and prospects another reason to join.

Using a cause as a branding strategy should not be undertaken merely to create a sense of sympathy for the organization and to attract new members. Choose the cause with the intent of making a commitment to improving or changing the industry, community, profession, or society. It would do a great disservice to your organization, its members, and the cause to undertake this type of effort with anything less than the most positive of motives. Once that decision is made, however, use the cause to expand your branding efforts. Being associated with a worthy cause can add to your organization's credibility and reputation.

Several membership organizations have successfully used causes to add to their brand identification. Rotary International, a membership service organization based in Evanston, Ill., has more than 2,500 affiliated clubs worldwide. It began as a business networking organization; local businesspeople met regularly to share ideas and develop contacts. Early on, Rotary International realized there had to be more to the organization than business people having lunch once a month to share ideas and tips. The group encouraged its clubs to adopt service projects in their local communities. This effort attracted more members and gave some additional programming focus to the local clubs. This ideal of local community service, however, didn't brand Rotary as anything other than another service group. In short, there was no exclusivity.

Rotary undertook a major effort to brand itself, to solidify its image as an important organization, and to help focus the energies of its members. It took on the challenge of working

Adopting a Cause

In the private sector, the Wendy's hamburger corporation has used several methods to establish its brand identity. Wendy's started off with an identifiable image—a redheaded girl in a dress who was Wendy herself (actually the daughter of Dave Thomas, the company's founder). Then the company added its "fresh and juicy" slogan to the logo so consumers would associate the two images— the redheaded girl meant fresh and juicy hamburgers. The slogan also attempted to create an "exclusivity" feature: Although other companies served hamburgers, only Wendy's served fresh and juicy hamburgers.

After Wendy's became a success, Dave Thomas added another aspect to the company's public image—identification with a cause. An adopted child himself, Thomas used Wendy's brand identification to promote adoption and adoption services. While Thomas didn't become active in adoption causes just to sell hamburgers, his activity in that area brought additional attention to his company and created a deeper, more positive image in the minds of customers and potential customers.

to eradicate polio throughout the world. Of course, Rotary wasn't the first or only organization to identify polio as a cause and to undertake programs to combat the disease— but it branded itself as the organization that had assumed a major role in the fight. Over the years, Rotary not only became noted and notable for its efforts in the overall fight against polio but also became synonymous with that effort in many local communities.

Did this effort to brand the organization attract more members? Perhaps. More important, however, is that Rotary's affiliation with the polio cause helped create a more positive membership environment. The image of Rotary made it easier for membership recruiters to open conversations with prospective members. Rotary had an excellent set of membership values to market—the tangible, business-related values of networking and the additional value of making a difference in people's lives. In a similar fashion, Lions International adopted vision care as its cause and has become known for its eye banks and related activities.

Another membership organization that uses a cause to help create a brand identity is the American Medical Association Alliance (AMAA), Chicago. Started as a support group for the American Medical Association (AMA), AMAA's membership was composed of the spouses (almost all wives) of AMA members. For much of its history, AMAA was known as the American Medical Association Auxiliary.

In the old marketplace, AMAA had a positive image and reached a membership high of 90,000. Then the new marketplace began to take its toll. As the spouse supporting her physician husband gave way to the new, busy, career-oriented spouse with little time and multiple priorities, AMAA's membership started to drop. AMAA had a brand identity; the problem was it had the wrong brand identity. When potential members heard the words "American Medical Association Auxiliary" the image came to mind of doctors' wives holding social functions. In truth, AMAA had always been active in grassroots politics, promoting better health, and supporting the goals of organized medicine. The organization had been branded as something other than what it was.

To stem the loss in membership, AMAA first changed its name from Auxiliary to Alliance. The organization wanted to communicate that it was an independent partner with AMA, not a subjugated afterthought. This matched the changing image physicians' spouses had of themselves. The name change alone created interest among prospective members.

In addition, AMAA decided to become identified with a purpose or cause that was more focused than simply assisting AMA and its affiliates. AMAA chose to become involved with the effort to reduce violence in America. It developed a series of programs to encourage public awareness of violence, as well as specific programs its affiliates could undertake to change public policy. This combination of education and action gave the alliance a new focus. To further brand itself, AMAA named its program SAVE—Stop America's Violence Everywhere.

The organization could now recruit members with a set of membership values that included both its traditional values and its new cause. The goal was to attract members by changing the image—from a group of doctors' wives getting together once in a while to a community-based action group working to improve public health and stop violence. Two quite different images, two quite different recruiting environments.

Step 5: Brand Through Identification with Quality

In some ways, this step is closely aligned with the Total Quality Management (TQM) business process that gained attention in the late 1980s and early 1990s. Some aspects of that era continue to affect business in general and membership organizations specifically.

In the United States, two aspects of TQM have endured. First is the idea that customers should expect, even demand, quality from every provider of products or services. The line from the movie *Network* was revived and used repeatedly— "I'm mad as hell, and I'm not going to take it any more." Part of the process of improving quality in business, consumers were told, was to demand quality—and demand it loudly. The TQM movement was a response to this customer-driven demand and meant that everyone expected a higher quality of service from every source, including membership organizations. The quality of the products and services provided by membership organizations was now being judged, more than ever before, against the quality of products and services from private providers.

Although the TQM movement helped increase the standards for all providers, it also put many membership organizations in a new position. Members were no longer willing to overlook lapses in quality out of sympathy for the fact that not-for-profit organizations didn't have the resources to compete with private firms. Everyone had learned to expect more and better service, and membership organizations were not getting a free ride anymore.

The second enduring aspect is the TQM concept of measurement criteria. Quality moved from being an attitude and a slogan to a measurable business function. This put pressure on membership organizations to establish standards of quality for everything they did—a new challenge for groups that had always counted on the loyalty and goodwill of their members to allow them to produce programs, products, and services that may not have been at the same level as those provided by a for-profit.

These two carryover effects of the TQM era provide opportunities for membership organizations as they create brand identification in the new marketplace. They can use quality as a cornerstone of branding efforts by promoting the *institutionalized* quality of everything they do, especially in regard to member service, communications, and responsiveness. This commitment to quality brands the organization as one that is aware of member expectations and has made a commitment and has developed a system to meet and exceed those expectations.

In the area of measurement criteria, organizations can now support their claims of quality with proof. By using quality control measurements to brand themselves, organizations create the image they want with members and potential members. Quality measurement criteria include:

- Number of consecutive months of publishing a magazine or newsletter on time.
- Average length of time a caller spends on hold.
- Response time to inquiries or requests for information.
- Average time a member waits in line to register for a meeting.
- Amount of time from receipt of membership application to the first contact from the organization.

- Number of complaints about speed, service, accuracy, or attitude.

Each measurement provides an opportunity for the organization to brand itself: It knows what quality is and can substantiate its success in providing quality products and services to its members.

Step 6: Understand the Challenges of Creating a Brand Image

All organizations face challenges when trying to establish a brand identity with various publics. Not-for-profit membership organizations face unique challenges because of their unique nature.

Pricing strategies. The price of any product or service is always a major consideration. Membership organizations have to determine whether it is to their advantage to be identified as the "cheapest" provider. If so, how does the organization maintain the perception of quality?

Some private providers brand themselves as "the best, not just the cheapest," which makes members wonder if their organization can match the quality of the private firm at a lower price. On the other hand, if the membership organization decides to charge more for a product or service to maintain the quality level, it risks being perceived as too expensive.

The pricing strategy dilemma for membership organizations arises from the fact that they are, by definition, not-for-profit. Charging high prices for membership, products, and services may brand them as organizations driven by profits, which would diminish the member loyalty built up over many years. Some members assume membership organizations will offer products and services at *lower* prices because the organization simply needs to break even on its activities. Although this is rarely the situation, the assumption adds to the effect that price has on an organization's image.

The growing number of competitors. Multiple competitors from the for-profit, government, and not-for-profit sectors stretch a membership organization's resources and credibility. As more entities brand themselves with images similar to those of membership organizations—especially in the areas of products and services rather than causes or missions—membership organizations will find it more difficult to brand themselves via exclusivity.

The danger of too much information. Information overload is another characteristic of the millennium marketplace. As members and potential members continue to be overwhelmed by the amount and flow of information and the number of choices they have, branding campaigns may fail simply because their messages get lost in the information clutter. When consumers (or members and prospects) are bombarded with an ever-growing number of images, they tend to stay with the most familiar ones. It is harder to change your organization's image in this environment. The information clutter adds to the challenge of standing out and being considered unique.

Time and money pressures. Membership organizations typically don't have the financial resources of private companies or even government services, which can increase exposure by staying with a branding campaign longer in an effort to overcome the overload of information and images. Budgetary restraints often force membership organizations to reach their goals more quickly, shorten the program's length, or revise their goals. The organization may have been close to accomplishing its brand identification goals but can't see the project through to completion.

Private-sector companies can sometimes absorb "loss leader" programs for the sake of long-term goals. This is not always the case in membership organizations, where there is generally an element of volunteer input in a branding effort (as in all programs). In addition to the financial pressures to complete an image-building campaign, the organization may be encouraged to shorten the time frame to coincide with the end of a particular program or budget year. Or there may be pressure to complete branding efforts before the end of a leader's term of office.

Unfortunately, when these pressures come into play, membership organizations may not see their branding efforts through to a conclusion. Starting a branding program and ending it prematurely can create just the opposite image from the one the organization wanted to project. A shortened or revised program can leave the targeted publics with mixed messages and fragments of images. Any branding campaign must be planned out carefully and carried out fully.

Step 7: Establish clear and reasonable goals for the program

As with any program, branding efforts need to be accompanied by credible measurement criteria. With any image-building program, there may be a tendency to believe measurement is impossible; after all, how do you get into the minds of the targeted publics and see the organization as they do?

The subjective, rather than quantitative, approach can be especially dangerous when volunteer leaders are involved. These leaders often don't view the organization as a true business because profit doesn't drive it, so they are willing to make subjective decisions about a program's value. Volunteer leaders are also prone to avoiding tightly defined measurement criteria because they don't want the accountability (and accompanying disappointment) if the program fails.

Here are suggestions for measurement criteria that could apply to your organization's branding efforts.

Membership retention. Can the image of the organization be related directly to the percentage of members who renew each year? Of course. If one objective of the branding campaign is to raise the stature of the organization in the minds of members and prospective members, the membership retention rate should be a basic measurement.

It will be difficult to determine if the branding efforts are the *only* reason for improved retention, but certainly some aspect of retention can be attributed to these efforts. In the private sector, this measurement would be called repeat customers, or customer loyalty.

Member awareness. Another measurement of effectiveness answers this question: Does your organization have a higher name and image recognition than it did before the branding efforts started?

To measure the effect of the program, a baseline or starting measurement needs to be established. Determine your organization's name recognition in the current marketplace so you can track the upward or downward trends in the future. A survey of current members, prospects, and other targeted publics will establish this baseline. For example, a survey might ask what image or product respondents associate with your organization's name or marketing slogan. The survey can measure such areas as who has heard of the organization or slogan and, if so, what connotations the name or image has (good, bad, indifferent, high quality, and so forth).

After establishing this baseline information, create a branding campaign to change the current images into the desired images. After the campaign has been in place for a specified period, conduct a new survey and compare the results to the previous survey and to the goals established for the program. Make adjustments, where necessary, to keep the program focused and on track for attaining its stated goals.

Membership growth versus competing organizations. If your organization knows where its membership stands in relation to competing organizations in its field, trade, or community, you can gauge the success of branding efforts by determining how many prospective members are joining it rather than a competing organization.

Membership retention during dues increases. While membership retention rates are a basic measurement of branding effectiveness, a more specific measurement is the retention rate during a cycle in which a dues increase has been implemented. If your organization can keep its retention rates up during a dues increase, it must have done a good job convincing members that its programs and products are so valuable and of such high quality that they are worth having at a higher price.

The concept of product branding isn't new, yet it has not been employed effectively by membership organizations in the past. In the new marketplace, membership organizations will need to use every available technique to get their message out to members and prospective members. Branding should be one of those techniques.

CHAPTER 6

Create a Membership Experience

To UNDERSTAND THE NEW MEMBERSHIP marketplace, it's necessary to look outside the scope of membership organizations. You can learn a lot about the attitudes of members in the millennium marketplace from something as simple as, say, the purchase of a fence.

What does buying a fence have to do with why someone might choose to join (or rejoin) a membership organization? Take a closer look, and you'll learn some lessons from this seemingly insignificant transaction, one described in "A Tale of a Fence, or the Death of Commodities," an article published by the American Management Association in *American Management Review* (November 1996).

Written by economist Oren Harari, the article told how the author wanted to purchase a fence to surround his swimming pool and protect his young son. After the fence was installed, he thought it wasn't adequate, so he asked the contractor to make some modifications. The contractor insisted he had built the fence to specifications but would gladly make any

Key Points

The new marketplace challenges organizations to create a membership experience that members can relate to at retention time. Creating a positive membership experience—the total of all interactions the member has with the organization—requires instituting a system that will connect with members and encourage them to spread the word about the value of membership. The key steps include:

1. **Combine technologies to create member friendly interactions with the organization.**

2. **Ensure everyone who deals with members realizes that he or she is part of the membership experience.**

3. **Remember the member/prospect begins making value judgments with the first contact.**

4. **Don't blame members if they don't know how your organization can help them.**

5. **Never believe you have 12 months to convince members to renew.**

6. **Surprise members at least twice a year by doing something they don't expect.**

7. **Strive to be the first to reach your members with everything.**

8. **Personalize as much of the member interaction as possible.**

9. **Always close the loop on member communications.**

10. **Ask the right questions.**

changes as long as Harari could say specifically what he wanted done and, of course, pay for the changes.

Harari wrote, "In the old order of things, this was simply a matter of the customer and the vendor seeing things differently. In the **new order,** however, things are different. I thought I wanted a fence because I could envision it, but what I really wanted was a *solution to my problem.* Nowadays, customers are more demanding and fickle than ever before. They have more choices, from increases among vendors for almost all products and services, all the way to the self-help possibilities of the

World Wide Web. Hence, they will gravitate toward vendors who understand that *business is no longer about buying and selling products and services. It is about addressing people's motives and desires.* Most businesses today are run with absolutely no understanding of this point."

He might have added that many membership organizations are run with no understanding of this point, either. People who contact membership organizations might say they want a publication when they really want data on industry trends. They say they'd be willing to serve on a committee but what they really want is a chance to meet some community business leaders.

Later in his article Harari concludes, "In the new order what will count for customers is the **total experience** they have with the vendor. They will judge the vendor on things like how easy was it to work with the vendor, does the vendor really understand what *I'm* looking for, how responsive is the vendor, is the vendor willing to adjust to my demands, and *how effective is the vendor at solving my problems.*"

He could have substituted the word "member" for the word "customer," and the word "organization" for the word "vendor," without changing the meaning of the statement. The concept of the total experience is a basic one for membership recruitment and retention in the new millennium.

Harari makes another point that describes a challenge facing organizations in the new marketplace: "Simply listening to the customer and then responding will no longer be sufficient because the *customer may not be able to articulate what he or she really wants.*"

An Exercise in Frustration

Here is an example of how Harari's thoughts come to life every day in membership organizations.

A member called an organization's office just after closing time on a Friday afternoon. He was greeted with the following recorded message:

> Thank you for calling the XYZ organization. Our offices are now closed. Our regular business hours are 8:30 a.m. to 5 p.m., Eastern Standard Time, Monday through Friday.
>
> If you are calling from a touchtone phone and wish to leave a message, touch 1 now. If you know your party's extension, dial it now. If you know your party's name, dial it now starting with the first three letters of the person's last name. For a directory of our staff, dial 3 now. If you want to talk to the membership department, touch 4 now. If you want to talk to the convention department, touch 5 now. If you want to talk to the finance department, touch 6 now. If you want to talk to the education department, touch 7 now. If you want to talk to the chapter relations department, touch 8 now. If you wish to leave a message in our general mailbox, touch 9 now and a staffer will get back to you as soon as possible.

At first, this seems like a typical contact with an organization that isn't open. After all, no one expects the organization's office to be open all the time. However, this simple example of a "menu" message shows how many opportunities the organization missed.

- It's essential to remember is that it's not about the organization. It's about the member. Members calling the organization have a problem or a question they need answered now. They become frustrated listening to so many options, especially if they're calling long distance. The recorded message basically tells them that the best to hope for is a return phone call in three days. How many members will wait that long before seeking other solutions to their problems?

- Although the organization's menu seems to give the caller every option possible, it makes some risky assumptions. Suppose callers don't know the last name of the party to whom they wish to speak? They can't spell it out. The staff directory does them no good unless they already know who they want to contact. Even if they know the appropriate person, they'll hear yet another recorded message with instructions on how to leave a voice mail message for the person (who obviously isn't there).

- Providing a directory of departments is no more helpful than a list of staffers if callers don't know what department might have the answer to their questions. Besides, after listening to all eight choices, callers may not remember which extension goes to what department. The only option is to start all over again, which may entail another long-distance call. It's getting very frustrating by this time.

In this case, the caller decided to access the organization's Web site to get the help needed. When the member located the organization's home page, here is what he found:

- A large, colorful banner welcoming the user to the Web site.
- A three-paragraph history of the organization.
- An advertisement for the organization's upcoming technical session.
- A place to click if the user wanted to join the organization.
- A listing of all of the organization's departments.

What's wrong with a home page that has all of this information? Nothing, provided the caller knows what department he or she needs, isn't a member and is interested in joining, wants to know the organization's history, or happens to be interested in the technical session being advertised.

Unfortunately, the organization's home page amounts to nothing more than its telephone menu in visual form. Neither is a help to the caller, who is looking for assistance with answering a question or solving a problem. Instead of listening to a voice message and pushing the correct extension, the

Web site user has to look through all of the choices and click on the correct one. After a few clicks—and after waiting for the graphics and copy to appear on the computer screen—the member has probably become so frustrated that he or she has turned off the computer.

All of this frustration builds up and can manifest itself in a bad attitude, poor word-of-mouth discussion about the organization, and possibly a dropped member at renewal time.

Adding It All Up

The preceding scenario is probably being repeated hundreds of thousands of times each day in membership organizations around the world. The result is that the member has now added this frustrating interaction with the organization to his or her membership experience.

The membership experience is the *total perceived experience* the member has with your organization. When the membership experience includes one or more frustrating interactions, such as those noted above, a member is likely to react in one of four ways.

- Contact the organization (by waiting until Monday morning, of course) and explain his or her frustration. The member might also suggest how the organization might have been able to be of more help.

- Do nothing. The member may assume this is the best the organization can do, given its small budget and resources, and forget about the incident.

- Seek other ways to solve the problem, rather than waiting for the organization to figure out that he or she is frustrated and looking for help.

- Release his or her frustration by telling others—members and nonmembers—about the incident.

In the old marketplace, the first and second options were most likely. In the new marketplace, the third and fourth options are almost ensured. In fact, customer service surveys reveal that when people have a problem getting good service, only one in 10 will ever contact the organization to communicate his or her disappointment and frustration. These same surveys also reveal that the remaining nine out of 10 people—those who won't tell the organization—*will* tell an average of 13 others about their bad experience.

Three conclusions can be drawn from these statistics:

- For every complaint your organization receives from a member or prospect about an experience he or she has had, as many as nine others have had an experience just as frustrating but have never told you.

- For each of these nine people who also had a bad experience but never contacted your organization, as many as 13 other members or prospects have had a "second hand" bad experience.

- *No* membership organization can expect to survive in the millennium marketplace with such membership statistics working against it.

Positive Experiences

To successfully attract and keep members in the millennium marketplace, organizations will need to create a positive membership experience for all of their members. Here are 10 suggestions for doing that.

1. Combine technologies to create member friendly interactions with the organization

Short of having a staff person on call, how could the organization in the above example have reduced frustration for the member? In fact, the organization *had* an option, but didn't use it effectively—its Web site. However, never during the phone message did the organization mention its Web site, assuming the caller would know about the site and access it if necessary.

This is a faulty assumption, on at least two counts. First, why would the organization assume all callers would know it has a Web site? Not all callers are members, and not even all members know about the Web site. Second, suppose the caller doesn't know or remember the Web site's address? There's no guarantee that all members can search the World Wide Web and find the specific site they seek. If they have to search the Web to identify the organization's site, it might be faster to answer their original question by looking elsewhere on the Web and not bother with the organization at all.

The organization could have used the after-hours call as an opportunity to show the member how eager it is to help at all times. Combining telephone technology and Web site technology could have helped solve the member's problem, as this revised scenario illustrates.

The member calls the organization office and hears this message:

> Thank you for calling the XYZ organization. Although our offices are currently closed, we may still be able to help you with a solution to your problem or an answer to your question. If you need immediate help or information and have access to the Internet, please visit our Web site at www.organization.org. On the Web site you will find answers to our most frequently asked questions, a problem-solving guide, and a complete listing of our staff phone extensions and e-mail addresses.
>
> If you'd prefer to leave a message and do not need an immediate response, please touch 1 for our listing of voice-mail options. Once again, our 24-hour Web site assistance is available at www.organization.org, or press 1 to leave a voice mail message for one of our staff associates.

This second message improves on the first one in several ways.

- It creates empathy within the first few words by acknowledging that the caller may be frustrated at not having anyone to talk to about his or her problem.

- It says clearly that the organization does have help available, even if it is not a human being at the end of the telephone line.

- It gives the caller options by offering more than one way to get help with a question or problem.

Perhaps most important, the second message gives the caller control over the interaction. If a caller's only option is to listen to the organization's menu and follow the instructions carefully, the organization is in control of the call. One of the most intimidating feelings for a human being is feeling that someone else is in control of his or her behavior. Members can feel intimidated every day by work, by the government, and so on; they don't want that same feeling from an organization of which they are a member. They don't want to "pay" for the privilege of having someone else control them.

If the caller in this second scenario chooses to use the organization's Web site, here is what he or she needs to see on the home page.

- A welcome to the organization.

- A quick explanation of how to use the Web site.

- A place to click for telephone extensions and e-mail addresses of key staff members or leaders. (The e-mail listings should allow the user to send a message without having to leave the Web site.)

- A section titled "Most Frequently Asked Questions."

- A "Problem Solver" directory, listing key words, phrases, and descriptions. Examples: "Click here if you have a problem or question related to patient care," "Click here for statistical data and industry averages," and "Click here to access information about your specialty area."

This last section assures the user that your organization understands the problems its members face every day and can provide fast, easy assistance in some of those areas. To develop this problem-solving section, you can use the results of the research done to create a market segmentation and targeting chart (see Chapter 3).

Use every tool available to meet member needs and expectations. If your organization uses multiple technologies as part of its operations (including phone, fax, e-mail, and a Web site), use those same technologies—in any combination necessary—to recruit, serve, and retain members.

2. Ensure everyone who deals with members realizes he or she is part of the membership experience

Organizations make a big mistake when they assume that only those members and staffers who are directly involved with membership recruitment and retention are responsible for creating the membership experience. In fact, the list of people who create the membership experience goes beyond those who work for the organization or serve it in a leadership role.

Because *every contact* with the organization is part of the membership experience, every person or entity who *represents* the organization becomes part of the membership recruitment and retention team. From the receptionist who answers the phone to the staff person who answers questions, from the insurance company whose product is endorsed by the organization to the overnight courier service used to deliver packages to members, a widespread team of people creates the membership experience.

In the new marketplace, organizations must make sure that all of these people understand their role in the membership experience. Those in charge of the organization's membership development functions can't assume that everyone understands these roles.

3. Remember the member/prospect begins making value judgments with the first contact

When does the membership experience start? Most people would say it starts when the person or company joins the organization. Unfortunately, this is not the case.

Members and prospects start making judgments about your organization with their first contact. No matter who initiates the contact, the member starts making a mental list of whether it's worth joining or retaining membership in the organization. What first impression might prospects or members have of your organization if they encounter frustrating voice-mail menus and confusing Web sites? They already may be skeptical of the value of membership, and incidents like these aren't reassuring.

The speed of response is another factor, so it is important to understand what the members or prospects expect before determining how to meet and exceed those expectations. If the first contact a prospect has with an organization is asking for membership literature, even this simple order fulfillment can influence his or her attitude toward joining. By putting literature in the mail, you send the message that it takes three days for members to receive a response from your organization. If the membership person is unavailable and the prospect is told someone will call him or her back, you're sending the message that only one person in your organization can answer membership questions or send information. While none of these is true—it doesn't always take three days to get information, and anyone can send membership information—the membership experience indicates otherwise. The first contacts with people will determine their opinion about the organization, so you have to set standards and guidelines for initial interactions with members and potential members.

4. Don't blame members if they don't know how your organization can help them

Many organizations respond to telephone callers with a basic, simple, and friendly greeting such as, "Thank you for calling. How may we help you?" Unfortunately, the caller may not *know* how you can help. When asked "How may we help you?" the caller has to choose how to respond and how to direct the organization to help. When he or she receives an automated menu of choices, the decision of where to next ask for help becomes harder.

Avoid the temptation of becoming impatient or frustrated with members and prospects who don't know what they want. It's not their fault. Many times they don't know if the help they need exists within your organization. That's why they call—to find out if help is available. What does the caller know? He or she knows what problems need solving. Giving the prospect a list of product choices isn't the same as solving a problem.

5. Never believe you have 12 months to convince members to renew

As important as the first contact is, the membership experience continues beyond that point. Once a member joins, you usually have 12 months of interaction with that person before the renewal decision arises. Even a bad first impression can be overcome in those months if the organization is attuned to member needs.

Still, you don't have a full year to convince the person to renew just because that's the length of his or her membership. People aren't inclined to wait 12 months for an organization to prove its value.

Most organizations have a policy governing when they drop unpaid members from their membership rolls. When the drop date arrives, the organizations determine how many members they lost and calculate how many must be recruited to replace them. In some cases the organizations contact dropped members to find out why they didn't return. Typically, dropped members are defined as those who fail to pay their dues.

In reality, the point of nonrenewal is when your organization *finds out* that the member has dropped. The member may have dropped out in his or her mind months ago. The organization first learns about the decision to drop when it asks for another year's dues.

It's this gap between the time a member decides to drop and the time your organization finds out about it that causes problems that could be avoided by having a systematic member retention program in place. Even members who renew year after year make mental lists of the membership experience. In the millennium marketplace, the burden falls on the organization to keep in touch with its members using technology, hard work, and common sense.

6. Surprise your members at least twice a year by doing something they don't expect

With so much competition for members' attention and loyalty, membership organizations need to stand out from the crowd. Fortunately, membership organizations have an advantage: Their members remain connected to them through regular communications vehicles (newsletters, magazines, faxes, and so forth). The contact continues even when the member is not being asked to buy something. Private-sector competitors need an excuse or permission to communicate with people—membership organizations don't.

Use this advantage to stand out from the other providers of services and products. This might entail taking risks and being less conservative than in the past. If people end up on solicitation mailing lists without paying for the privilege, why would they join an organization just to receive more mailings?

If they can get anything they want without joining, why would they?

If your organization can't compete on speed, price, or resources, it must compete on service and empathy. That means creating a feeling among members that your organization cares about them as something other than a source of revenue. To do that, surprise members by doing the unexpected, such as contacting them simply to say "Hi" or "Thank you." A personal contact, whether via letter, fax, e-mail, or a telephone call, goes above and beyond what members normally expect. A phone call, for instance, might go as follows:

"Hi, Ms. Smith. This is Charlotte Jones from the XYZ organization. We were updating our records and noticed you have been a member for almost six years now. I just wanted to call to let you know we really appreciate your continued membership and support. Don't forget that we're here to help you, so don't hesitate to contact us at any time. Have a great day."

If that sounds too artificial or overly enthusiastic for your organization, think about the call from the member's perspective. You didn't ask for any money or time, the call itself took only a few seconds, there was no ulterior motive, and you recognized the member for supporting the organization.

This technique is being used by a growing number of manufacturers and other product providers, who are making "thank you" calls to their customers. These calls will help the vendor when these customers are asked to buy that next product or service. If customers associate not only good products but also good service, good follow up, and personalized contact with a vendor, they are much more receptive to future sales approaches.

7. Strive to be the first to reach your members with everything

The ability to respond rapidly and provide information in a timely manner are two elements of effective member service that members regularly evaluate. If, like most not-for-profits, your organization can't afford new technologies to improve the speed of response, consider another way to compete: Make information on new innovations and trends available to members *before* the competition does.

Membership organizations are in a unique position to do this, because many innovations and trends within an industry, profession, or community exist *because* of them. Associations, chambers of commerce, professional societies, and other not-for-profit groups are in the forefront of industry or professional standards, statistical information, and so forth. Membership organizations are trend setters, even though they may not control access to all of the information or resources available.

For example, an organization may, through member surveys or statistical gathering, identify a need in the marketplace for a new product or service. The organization doesn't necessarily have to provide the service or produce the product. Its role might be to raise the awareness of its members (and other publics) about the need for the product or service and its availability through other (nonorganizational) sources. The point is that the organization alerted its members to an issue before anyone else did. This action creates the image that the organization keeps up on the latest information and gets it to members before other sources do.

In many cases, it is better to be the first to present an idea, trend, or product. This does not mean your organization should give the impression it has knowledge of everything happening in the field or can be all things to all people. But keeping up with what's happening—and promoting your involvement in making those things happen—gives you a distinct advantage over organizations that merely repeat information already available through other sources.

Being the first to reach members and prospects helps attract and keep members for two reasons:

- Even if members eventually purchase the product or service from a source other than your organization, they will remember where they heard about it first. Members feel confident that belonging to your organization gives them an advantage over nonmembers.

- You create brand loyalty. Although a competing (and perhaps superior) service or product may be available through other sources, members have already started using your organization as their source and will be unwilling to change providers unless a compelling reason to do so arises.

For example, your organization may be the first in its field to provide educational programming on how to comply with a new government regulation. Perhaps your organization worked to have the regulation adopted or knows a lot about it because it opposed the regulation. In any case, other entities—government agencies, universities, or for-profit companies—will soon make information on this regulation available to the same market you've targeted. If your organization was first on the scene, however, targeted audiences will associate it with the issue. A university or private provider may eventually provide education related to the regulation at a lower cost, but by then your organization has branded itself as the leader in this field by being first.

8. Personalize as much of the member interaction as possible

Because members know the technology exists to personalize mailings, organizations must move beyond equating personalization with mail merging letters and communications. Although important, that part of personalization is just the beginning of connecting with the member.

Some organizations are reluctant to put members' names on all communications, even when they have the technical and administrative ability. The reasons they cite usually include:

- The organization is too big and the cost too great to personalize thousands of letters and other correspondence.

- Members have degrees, certifications, and other designations that may be omitted because of computer error or limitations.

- Some members have nicknames or use names other than those listed in the official records. Trying to personalize correspondence to these people can backfire because they will know the organization really doesn't know them.

- Some members have names that are gender neutral, which increases the risk of alienating someone through misuse of the name.

- A growing number of members come from other countries where their names are used differently. (In Asian countries, for instance, some names are written with the surname first.)

- Some organizations consider it improper to call members and prospects by their first names; in other organizations, it would be too formal to call members by anything other than their first names.

These are all legitimate concerns, but there are ways to overcome them. First, look at the cost of not personalizing membership communications.

- Members get the impression the organization doesn't know who they are.

- The organization looks less sophisticated compared to other entities that make the effort to personalize.

- Over the years, statistics have consistently shown that personalized correspondence is more widely read and gains

Getting Personal

Here are some methods to personalize interactions with members and avoid potential drawbacks.

- If cost is the obstacle, look closely at the real costs involved. First calculate the cost of personalizing the correspondence (setting up systems, printing personalized letters, and coordinating personalized correspondence with the correct envelope), and weigh that extra cost against the higher response rate (projected at up to 30 percent more). That comparison itself may determine the value of personalization.

- To reduce the cost factor in terms of time, money, and mistakes, use window envelopes so there is no chance of putting a personalized letter for one member in an envelope addressed to someone else. The address typed on the letter becomes the label for mailing purposes.

- To address the problem of inaccuracies, use a different format for writing to members and prospects. If you're concerned a prospect's name won't be printed accurately, print the entire, formal name and title onto a memo. A communication might read:

  To: Robert A. Jones, MD
  From: XYZ Organization
  Subject: Five Ways to Earn CME Credits at the Upcoming
           Conference

This method lets the computer read and print out the person's entire name and credentials, giving the recipient the credibility he or she wants. It also seems as though this message is specifically for this particular member. The rest of the message can easily be customized according to membership category or demographic segment.

Make sure you gather all the information needed to customize and personalize communications and add it to your membership database. For instance, on membership applications or renewal notices, you can include questions regarding members' preferences on how they wish to be addressed. This information needs to be updated periodically, but once it is captured in the information database it can be used in many ways.

a higher response rate than impersonal correspondence. According to direct mail specialists, putting a person's name on correspondence can result in a response rate as much as three times higher than "Dear member" correspondence.

People are already concerned about being lost in the crush of numbers and computerized systems. One competitive advantage membership organizations need to exercise is their ability to make members feel cared about as individuals with specific needs instead of generic customers who want a product or service. This feeling of individual importance should be an important part of the membership experience.

9. Always close the loop on member communications

Some membership organizations mistakenly equate effective member communications with the amount of information sent out to members. Others are content with two-way communication—the organization sends a message and the member responds. But truly effective communications require a continuous loop: The organization sends information, the member responds to the information, and the organization *acknowledges the member response.* This last step, which is often forgotten, offers another opportunity to create a unique membership experience. A membership organization should want to be the only product or service provider that goes the extra step to reassure members they are being listened to.

Many private firms and service providers have started using their communications and technology resources to respond to every interaction with customers by sending a confirmation. They close the communications loop, which has raised members' expectations; members look for the same concentrated follow-up from their organizations.

Consider the member survey—the way most organizations seek input on what the members want them to do or to provide. Asking members' opinions is one way to keep members involved, yet member surveys historically have had low response rates. The reason might be poor survey documents or bad timing. Or perhaps members don't return the surveys because they don't believe that the organization will listen to their opinions.

Most surveys provide a way for respondents to add specific ideas or suggestions to the questions asked. Let's say a member writes "a dental insurance program" in the blank space for suggesting new services. When the organization tallies the survey results, only that one member has suggested a dental program. Will the organization act on that suggestion immediately? Of course not. But the member doesn't know he or she was alone in making the suggestion. When the organization announces the survey results or its new programs, the dental program won't appear on the list. The only conclusion the member can draw is that the organization didn't listen to his or her suggestion—so what was the point of returning the survey? The next time a survey comes out, the disenchanted member is less likely to respond. Even worse, when the renewal invoice arrives, the member may drop out instead of paying dues to an organization that doesn't care what its members say.

In fact, someone did read the member surveys and note the suggestion about the dental plan. It was among the new programs discussed, but the low level of interest didn't warrant including a dental plan in the organization's list of programs or services. No one, however, told the member his or her suggestion was considered. No one closed the loop on the communication. The organization assumed it had done all it should by creating a two-way communication with the member. The organization sent out the survey, and the member responded. In this case, there was a need for a third communication—acknowledgment of the member's suggestion.

Was the organization obligated to implement the member's suggestion regarding the dental plan? Absolutely not. Was the organization obligated to tell the member what it did with his or her suggestion? Absolutely. Here's what the organization could have done:

- Asked anyone who made additional comments to sign the survey for the purpose of being contacted for follow-up information.

- Issued a summary report on the survey to all members, which included the write-in comments and an explanation of how the organization uses the comments.

Acknowledge member input as often—and as specifically—as possible. The example of the survey response is just one way to address the closing of the membership communications loop.

10. Ask the right questions

If membership becomes nothing more than a series of products and services, some group or person will come along eventually and provide those products and services better, faster, or cheaper than most membership organizations can. When that happens, the membership is in jeopardy.

That's why you must ask the right questions of members and prospects. "What do you want your organization to do for you?" is the wrong question. The right questions, like the programs and services provided by membership organizations, must focus on the member or prospect, not on the organization.

What problems do you need to have solved? Not all organizations or all situations call for the words "problem solving" because members don't always believe they have a problem. Maybe they just want information. But this question focuses the entire membership experience on the member. The right question must convey the organization's intent to be in business to assist and serve the member. If this intent can be communicated effectively and consistently, the membership experience will be a positive one, an experience the member will want to repeat.

What are your preferences? There is a difference between options and preferences. A member may have limited options for receiving information or participating in activities. Regardless of the number of options, always ascertain the member's *preferences*. An option is customer/member service from the *organization's* perspective (e.g., here are the ways we will let you get this service or product). Asking for the member's preference is customer service from the *member's* perspective—within our capabilities, you can get the product or service in the manner most convenient to you. In the future, making assumptions about members' preferences will prompt them to seek other sources of information and service. Even if members choose traditional options (in terms of communications systems, for example), being given a choice creates the impression that they can customize their membership to suit their individual needs.

What do you think? Asking for members' opinions is a basic and easy way to make them feel involved with the organization and, therefore, more likely to renew. Use every system imaginable—paper, fax, telephone, e-mail, Web sites—to solicit opinions. If the only interaction a member has during the year is being asked for an opinion, that may be enough to make the decision to renew. This assumes, of course, that your organization closes the loop and tells members how it used their opinions.

What talents would you like to contribute? By determining what members can do, and like to do, you can pinpoint ways for them to become more involved. When asking members to participate—not just in leadership positions but in many different ways—identify what they can accomplish by committing their time.

With time being the currency of the new millennium, it will be increasingly difficult to get a commitment from members without offering something in return: an estimate of how much time the activity will take and the outcome of that time expenditure. To make participation more attractive, match the activity to the member's interest and ability to accomplish something.

What are your communications capabilities? Members and prospects will develop various technological and communications capabilities at different times. Making assumptions about the ability of members to receive and send information at a specific level can lead to miscommunication. Instead, find out what members are capable of and communicate with them at their comfort level.

Looking Ahead

In the next century, the membership experience will become the frame of reference for members when they receive their renewal notices. It will no longer be a specific program, service, or activity that members will remember. They will judge the value of their membership by recalling the total experience of the previous year.

CHAPTER 7

50 Ideas That Can Help Retain Members in the Millennium Marketplace

THE FOLLOWING COMPILATION of retention ideas and activities was collected from many organizations. Some of these ideas will apply only to smaller organizations or perhaps to local chapters or affiliates of larger organizations, while others are more appropriate for larger organizations with greater resources.

This is not intended as a list of what to do or of the best ideas ever implemented—it's merely a list of options to consider when revising your organization's membership plan.

1. With the traditional welcome letter, send new members a thank-you note. Most organizations send new members a packet of information. Sending an additional letter gives you another chance to reiterate what a good investment the new members have made by joining. More personal and less formal than the form letter included in most new member packets, this communication could even be an e-mail message. For additional effect, this welcome letter should come from a member of the organization (perhaps an officer) rather than from the staff.

2. Include networking tips in your newsletter or new member packet. Survey results from various membership organizations indicate that networking is a primary reason for joining and one of the most important benefits to offer. To organizational leaders, networking usually means attending a function. However, some people—especially those who are new to an organization—are not comfortable with a room full of strangers. These people will sometimes attend an organizational function and come away feeling disappointed because they didn't meet anyone.

An experienced member would say the organization can only provide the networking opportunities, then it's up to individual members to do the actual networking. Why not help the member get the most out of these opportunities? Produce a short article or checklist on how to use these networking opportunities more effectively. Publish the list in your newsletter or magazine, add it to a meeting or convention brochure, or send it directly to members via mail or e-mail. Another option would be to fax the list to preregistered attendees shortly before the function. Among the tips included on this "effective networking list" might be:

- Bring plenty of business cards.
- Get a list of preregistered attendees before the meeting and pinpoint the people you want to meet.
- When exchanging business cards, always write one or two words on the back of the other person's card as a way of remembering who he or she was and what you discussed.

In addition to this checklist, the article should describe the meeting or function, including how registration will be handled and what is appropriate dress. The idea is to help attendees get the most out of their participation.

At each meeting there are probably several people who will not attend any more functions for the entire year. When these members receive their renewal notices, one of the first images that will come to mind is the meeting they attended.

If that image reminds them of a good meeting where a lot of contacts were made, you have a good chance of getting their renewal. But if the image is of a crowded room where the only meaningful conversation was among people who already knew each other, the chances for retention diminish.

3. When using testimonials, include some from members who aren't active but still feel membership is valuable. Empathy is the cornerstone of membership retention. If members feel as though the organization really understands their day-to-day challenges and is trying to help them cope with those challenges, they are more likely to renew. With members who have little contact with the organization, however, establishing empathy can be difficult. How does an organization express empathy to someone it never sees? Perhaps another member can establish that type of contact.

123

50 Ideas
That Can Help
Retain Members
in the Millennium
Marketplace

Identify members who are not very active but continue to renew, then ask them to contact other inactive members who are thinking of dropping out to explain the value of membership. This contact can take the form of a note or telephone call. Hearing from another member about the value of renewing, even when it is impossible to attend organizational functions, could help convince members that your organization is worth supporting.

4. Use "jeopardy marketing" to remind members of benefits. The term "jeopardy marketing" refers to "Jeopardy," a television quiz show popular in the United States for many years. The game show requires contestants to phrase their answers in the form of a question. Organizations can borrow this concept when explaining the value of membership to prospects. Here are a few samples of how to reword benefit statements using the technique of jeopardy marketing.

- Instead of saying, "Our organization offers lobbying and advocacy services," rephrase the statement as a question:

"Wouldn't it be great if someone were working every day to tell the public about the contributions our industry makes and to stand up for the rights of companies to practice in this field?"

- Instead of saying, "We offer a wide range of professional journals and other publications," ask "Wouldn't it be nice if every month someone brought to your door another form of continuing education and a place to find out about job openings?"

Using questions instead of answers allows readers to scan the material quickly. More important, this technique gets the member or prospect to mentally agree with the statements, and it creates the impression that the organization must have some empathy for the people reading the material.

5. Conduct focus groups by telephone, instead of asking people to travel to a central site. Focus groups are an effective way to gather information and to involve members, thereby increasing the probability of retention. Because of time constraints, however, people are finding it increasingly difficult to travel to a central location. Conference-call focus groups allow people to participate without traveling and in the setting they prefer (home or office).

When selecting participants, segment your membership. For example, a focus group could include members with varying years of experience in a field or companies of a certain size. This creates a true focus group by concentrating on the needs of a small segment. Also, be sure to select participants who are not active members or among the organization's leadership group. Organizations hear from active members all the time. Focus groups are an opportunity to ask some of the least active members how they feel.

When doing a focus group via telephone, remember the dynamics are different than in a meeting where everyone is in the same room. Here are some tips to ensure that telephone focus groups are as inclusive and productive as possible:

- Send all the participants an agenda and a set of rules before the call. The rules should include asking attendees to avoid distractions during the call (other phone calls, working on computers, and so on) and, if appropriate, to tell others in their workplaces not to disturb them.

- Take attendance at the beginning of the call to let everyone know who is participating.

- Ask participants to identify themselves each time they speak. It is not possible for everyone on a conference call to recognize other voices.

- The moderator should keep notes and record each time a participant speaks. A simple technique, such as making a small mark next to the person's name on an attendance list, works well. Keeping track of who participates allows the moderator to ask for input from specific people or ask that all participants respond to a topic. This prevents one or two people from dominating the discussion, which can distort the information gathered via the focus group method.

- After the focus group concludes, write or e-mail all of the participants to thank them for their input. This follow up should include a preliminary summary of the opinions expressed during the call and explain briefly how your organization will use the information gathered. This last point is crucial because it reminds the participants that the organization not only solicited their opinions but also listened to them.

6. Give an incentive—such as a free gift—to members who renew by a certain date. Many membership organizations offer prizes to members who recruit new members or to prospects who join during a designated period. These techniques are effective but can lead to resentment among existing members who may have joined when incentives

125

50 Ideas
That Can Help
Retain Members
in the Millennium
Marketplace

weren't offered. Rather than ignoring these feelings or telling members it is just a matter of timing, offer retention incentives to current members, such as a small discount on the dues paid by a certain date.

Another option is to offer free publications or reduced registration fees for future meetings or functions. While these incentives might not encourage more members to renew, they might prompt members who had planned to renew to do it sooner. This gives your organization a chance to identify potential drops earlier in the renewal process and allows it to have the interest-earning dues sooner.

7. Have a renewal lottery—if members renew before a certain date they qualify for a drawing for a big prize. Lotteries are popular, and members might be encouraged to renew (or renew more quickly) for the chance to win a specific prize. In most cases, the prize needs to be fairly substantial to convince members to renew early. Some examples of early renewal lottery prizes are a free year of membership the following year or free convention packages.

8. Communicate successes to members regularly— don't wait until the annual report. Many organizations produce an annual report or annual letter to show members what has been accomplished during the previous year. These reports are often included with renewal notices. By that time, the information doesn't have much effect on retention.

Rather than waiting until the end of the year, share success stories with members throughout the year. Remember, the membership experience is ongoing; it does not occur only at renewal time. Communicate with members whenever you have a story to tell, either in your publications or via e-mail, Web sites, and faxes. Faxing a summary of a success personalizes the message and shows members their organization is working every day, not just at renewal time.

9. Generate segmented and targeted renewal notices.
Tell each member segment how the organization benefited
them this year, preferably through a customized letter or
annual report. This doesn't mean leaving out some of your
organization's accomplishments but rather showcasing them
from the target group's perspective. It emphasizes that
members are individuals.

For instance, the report might be the same for all members
with the exception of one paragraph highlighting accomplishments that affected specific membership segments. A trade
group might say, "Although we believe all of our members
benefited from our successes in the past year, your firm gained
some special advantages in the marketplace because of our
work on the labor bill, the new training programs we sponsored, and the added section of our trade show." The benefits
would change slightly depending on what category the member
was in and what successes applied to people or companies in
that area.

**10. Send a special certificate of thanks to first-time
renewals.** During the first years of membership, members
form their initial judgments about the value of membership
and define the membership experience as created by the
organization. Statistically speaking, the first two years of
membership produce the vast majority of the annual drops,
so it makes sense to add special efforts for the retention of
these members.

When members renew for the first time, congratulate
them on making another good decision. Some organizations
list "First Time Renewals" or "First Anniversary Members"
in their publications, much as they do with new members. It
reinforces how glad the organization is that the member liked
the first year of membership and decided to renew.

This attention to first-time renewals also establishes a pat-
tern of member service. Saying thank you gets that member's
second year off to a good start. And if your organization can

127

50 Ideas
That Can Help
Retain Members
in the Millennium
Marketplace

keep members for at least two years, you have a good chance of keeping them for many more.

11. Identify and recognize members with the most tenure. Along the same lines as the "Member Since" idea is recognizing members who have been in the organization the longest. These are not people or companies likely to be dropping out, so giving them special recognition won't affect their decision to renew. By recognizing long-time members, however, your organization sends a message to those who might be contemplating dropping. The message is clear: If these successful companies have been members for so long, the organization has value. Maybe the member should reconsider the value of membership based on the longevity of these other members.

Recognition for long-time members need not be expensive or elaborate. The manner of recognition offered is of secondary importance. The fact the recognition is given is what matters.

12. Identify at least four specific contacts to make with first-year members that are above and beyond the norm. Four is a somewhat arbitrary number. The actual number of additional contacts made during the first year (versus the number of contacts made with members who have been in the organization longer) will vary from one organization to the next. In any case, plan a system for making contact during the first year. These additional contacts may take the form of phone calls, faxes, special newsletters, and so on.

If first-year members, those who are most vulnerable in terms of dropping their membership, are treated like every other member, your organization is not using its retention resources effectively. There is value in the long run by spending extra time and money in the short run (the first year).

13. Add ordering options to each item on your publications order form. The new marketplace is full of options. Whenever members interact with your organization, they want choices on how to create that interaction, whether it's attending a function or making a transaction. Even the simple act of ordering a publication contributes to the overall membership experience, so the transaction must be hassle free and positive. Remember, each interaction with your organization can be the basis for the member's decision to renew or drop.

Set up your fulfillment process so the member or customer can choose a preferred response method—for instance, overnight delivery, fax, regular mail, e-mail. Giving members payment and ordering options shows your organization is flexible and will go to great lengths to ensure members get what they want, when they want it, and in a format that meets their needs.

129

50 Ideas
That Can Help
Retain Members
in the Millennium
Marketplace

14. Develop a written retention plan. When asked to describe the basic steps in their retention plan, many organizations don't have a definitive answer. Their retention "plans" often consist of simply providing good service and systematically collecting dues. But to make changes that will increase membership retention, and to measure the effect of those changes, you need an identifiable plan.

The retention plan can be as simple or as complicated as you desire. The basic elements to include are retention goals (overall retention rate, retention rates by category, percentage of drops that were first-year members); corresponding current measurements in each goal area; specific activities to undertake to achieve those goals; identification of who is responsible for attaining these goals; resources available to implement the plan; and an indication of how frequently the plan and the results of its implementation will be reviewed and, if necessary, modified.

15. Do an e-mail survey of important questions and issues as they arise. When an important issue arises, the traditional procedure is to mail an announcement to all members and perhaps ask for a response (send a letter, make a call, contact a legislator). In today's marketplace, instead of merely informing members of the issue, organizations can solicit members' opinions or input via e-mail. E-mail surveys usually generate quick responses from members and also make them feel involved in the organization.

To make this involvement meaningful, use the e-mail survey technique randomly. It is not necessary to contact every member in the same way every time an important issue arises. In some cases, make contact with new members. In other cases, pinpoint your least active members and ask their opinion on a specific issue. Because not all members will have access to an e-mail system, substitute fax surveys for those without e-mail addresses.

16. Establish an Involvement Committee. This is another way to keep members involved in the membership process without requiring them to solicit new members. Or, it can be done in addition to having them recruit new members.

The purpose of this volunteer committee is to get members to participate in some way in the organization. If your organization has developed a member tracking system, the committee can pinpoint which members participate and which ones don't; those in the latter category become the first ones contacted by the committee. The tracking system also serves as a way of measuring the effectiveness of the Involvement Committee.

17. Involve the board in retention efforts. The health and growth of the organization is already among the board's responsibilities. For a different approach to that responsibility, divide the membership among the board and devise a retention system that awards points to board members for each member of their "team" during the year. (Example:

1 point if a team member attends a meeting, 1 point if a team member contributes to a foundation, 25 points when a team member renews). This may be practical for smaller organizations only, but larger groups may be able to use it through their chapters or affiliates.

The board member doesn't necessarily have to contact every member on his or her team and can certainly delegate some of the responsibility to other members (creating an opportunity for involvement). Contacts from the board member can come in the form of e-mails, faxes, or phone calls. The point is to get commitment from the top volunteer leaders to not only talk about the importance of member participation and retention but also do something about it.

18. Establish a member mentoring plan. Membership organizations can borrow the mentoring technique from the business world. As new members join, assign them to current members who will be their mentors during the first year of membership. Such a system ensures new members receive extra first-year contacts through a specific person, ensures the new member will have someone to contact about the organization and its benefits, and deepens the mentor's feeling of involvement with the organization (which can help retention).

19. Color code correspondence so members can quickly identify types of information. With various forms of information overwhelming the daily lives of members, organizations need their information to stand out in some way. Something as simple as color coding correspondence (one color for legislative news, one for educational information, and so forth) enables members to look through the material quickly, prioritize the information, and determine what information they want to handle first.

131

50 Ideas
That Can Help
Retain Members
in the Millennium
Marketplace

20. Institute a "thank you" column in your publication to recognize members for involvement and leadership. This is the paper version of the Heroes section on a Web site. Not all members have access to the Internet, but all receive organizational publications. Even organizations whose primary publications are technical in nature normally send one publication to members with information and updates. People love to see their names in print, even within a list of other names. The "Thank You" column could become a popular addition to your publication, with members looking at it immediately to see if their names, or those of people they know, are listed.

21. Send a member profile form to new members to gain information. Often, the application itself can be a barrier to membership, especially if it requests detailed demographic information. Lengthy applications take a long time to fill out and can frustrate the prospect. Make your membership application simple and quick to complete by asking for only the minimum information required by your organization's guidelines for acceptance. Don't let anything distract the applicant from the goal—completing the application.

To obtain more detailed information, send a simple follow-up New Member Profile form soon after a member joins. This form can be faxed or e-mailed back and the information added to the member profile database. This may seem like an extra step, one that could be avoided by asking for the information on the membership application, but it's another contact your organization can make during that crucial first year of membership. If a new member does not send the form back, this should be a sign that he or she may already be losing interest. Your organization can then add that member to the list of those who might need some mentoring or extra attention.

22. Have a special edition of your publication focus on how your organization is helping members prepare for the next century. Many people are facing the twenty-first century with trepidation. They feel unable to keep up with rapid change in their personal and professional lives and traditions and institutions seem to fall by the wayside every day.

Alleviate some of these fears and gain an additional level of member support by acknowledging the changes and helping members cope with them. The new century offers another opportunity to express empathy for members. By using organizational publications to customize the challenges of the new millennium and put them into a context relevant to members, you let members know someone is there is help them in times of radical change.

23. Be sure your Web page has hot links to individual members for business referrals and networking purposes. Take the lead in enabling people to meet and network electronically by designing a Web site that serves as an additional marketing tool for members. Most companies, and many individual practitioners, already have their own Web sites so it is a natural partnership for them to team up with their organization.

24. Offer a special listing in the directory to members who renew early. This incentive applies not only to printed directories but also to any online membership directory or roster your organization produces. It could be something as simple as giving all members who renew by a certain date larger typeface, bold lettering, or an asterisk next to their listings. Any incentive that encourages members to renew early helps an organization manage its retention efforts and invoicing system.

133

50 Ideas
That Can Help
Retain Members
in the Millennium
Marketplace

25. Keep experienced members active through targeted involvement. The success of membership organizations in the next century will depend, in part, on understanding the shifting priorities of the new generation of members. Newer (younger) members have different attitudes toward their organizations and different views on what they need. At the same time, another generation of members has led the organization up to this point. These older members still feel loyalty toward the organization but in some cases also feel pushed aside as the newer generation takes over leadership roles. Membership organizations need to keep both groups interested and involved.

In individual membership groups, when people feel their input is no longer valued, they start wondering about the value of the organization. In corporate membership organizations, the company representative is the key to "selling" the membership each year. If this representative loses interest in the organization, even if he or she has been an active member or leader, the organization is likely to lose its champion for continued membership. More threatening for corporate groups are mergers or acquisitions; the person who was previously active in the organization may not be assigned as the "new" company's representative. The danger at renewal time increases if the former representative feels the organization no longer values his or her input because he or she has been replaced by another representative.

To keep experienced members actively involved, and to help ensure their renewals, target involvement activities toward this group. These people are just as busy as other members, so keep the activities meaningful. Some of these people have already been through the chairs of leadership and are unlikely to be interested in starting over again by making large commitments of time. Here are a few suggestions for keeping these people active in and supportive of your organization.

- *Ask them to serve as mentors for newer members or newer leaders.* This mentoring can be as simple as an initial phone call after the assignment is made and occasional follow-up contacts or actually sitting down with newer members/leaders and guiding them through their first year.

- *Ask experienced members to write articles for your publications.* Even in the new millennium, publications will remain one of the most important benefits of belonging to a membership organization. Experienced members have a lot to share about their backgrounds, not only in the organization but also in their respective businesses or personal lives. Writing an article allows the member to participate with a limited time commitment; the work can be done whenever it is convenient for the member, and the job is over when the article is published. They will receive recognition for their efforts and feel a connection to the organization without being burdened by time-consuming committee work.

- *Ask experienced members and leaders to serve as liaisons to other organizations.* Tap past leaders to maintain contact with organizational partners, including other membership organizations, the media, civic organizations, coalitions, government agencies, and so on. The members can report back on the partners' current activities and opportunities for improving relationships with these other entities. This involvement usually doesn't entail a great deal of time but is still an important role, which gives the experienced member a continuing sense of accomplishment.

135

50 Ideas
That Can Help
Retain Members
in the Millennium
Marketplace

26. If your organization has corporate members, develop a system to involve top management of those companies. In individual member organizations, target top management in firms that employ large numbers of members. In the new millennium, members will face more pressure to justify the money spent on membership organizations as well as the time spent participating in them. As mergers and buy-outs continue worldwide, new managers coming into companies often have little knowledge of the organizations in which their employees are actively involved. To prevent a breakdown of support within these firms, target key member firms or employers and develop a system to solidify the support of those companies. Some techniques to consider:

- Executive Briefings, where a representative of the membership organization (either a staff person, volunteer leader, or both) makes a brief presentation to the senior management of the targeted firms. During the presentation the organizational representatives remind the managers of not only how much the company puts into the organization but also what the company receives in return for its support. The description of benefits should be specific and customized for the company and its needs.

- A series of executive profiles and interviews in your publications. One group ran a monthly column called The View From the Top, which featured a different chief executive officer of an important company giving his or her views on the industry, profession, or community. These interviews were usually done via telephone or through written questionnaires and, when published, included photos and background information on the CEO.

- Ask some key CEOs to serve on a panel at one of your meetings. One organization promoted this session as "100 Years of Experience" because the three CEOs collectively had been in the industry or profession more than a century. The attendance was high (possibly because employees of the CEOs' companies felt obligated to attend), and the peer pressure of having other CEOs on the panel was instrumental in getting a commitment from the panel members to speak. Most important, it gave these CEOs a favorable feeling about the organization and helped to solidify their support of their employees' involvement.

• Institute a "Five Deep Marketing Plan" in targeted companies, which means the firm has no fewer than five people in your organization's communications system. Not all of these people have to be dues-paying members. Should one or two people leave the firm, your organization is less likely to lose a member or corporate support because you still have contacts there.

137

50 Ideas
That Can Help
Retain Members
in the Millennium
Marketplace

27. Produce materials that clearly show what the company/employer gains by joining and participating in your organization. At times you may have to take the extra step and give members some help in "selling" the value of membership to their employers. Some groups have been very blunt about the message (for example, producing a brochure titled "How to Get Your Employer to Pay Your Dues"). Others have taken a low-key approach aimed directly at the employer (a brochure titled "What's in It for You to Sponsor a Member"). Regardless of the approach taken, show empathy for the members who have to justify their membership and participation to others.

This area lends itself to customization. Organizations can produce materials that delineate specific benefits for a particular type of company, industry segment, or specialty practice. Customization gives members a stronger message to take back to their employers.

28. For members recruited during a membership drive, add at least one extra contact during their first year of membership. No matter what they're called—member-get-a-member campaign, growth campaign, and so forth—membership drives are concentrated efforts to recruit new members over a specified period. Most efforts include an incentive for the new member who joins, for the current member doing the recruiting, or for both.

These drives may not remain effective in the new marketplace. If time is the most precious commodity to current members, persuading them to commit to a time-intensive membership drive may not be easy. Membership drives in the future may look different because of advances in technology and communications advances, but they will probably still be around.

What *will* change is the challenge to retain the members who join during these membership drives. Statistics gathered over the past few decades indicate that a higher percentage of members recruited during membership campaigns drop out after their first year of membership, compared to members who were recruited during other times of the year. Members recruited during membership campaigns are already among the highest-risk members, and in the new marketplace they certainly won't wait 12 months for your organization to prove its value.

Prepare to deal with higher, faster expectations by making sure every membership drive includes a well-defined and well-planned follow-up system for contacting prospects who didn't join during the campaign but remain good prospects and for staying in touch with the former prospects who did join. The retention of new members should begin the moment they join, and those who are at higher risk for dropping after the first year should receive specialized treatment.

Although the type of follow up will vary from one group to the next, several elements should be part of any program:

- Initiate a direct contact in addition to a welcome letter or new member packet. One of the first contacts made after a member joins should come from another human being.

- "Tag" members in the database as having joined during a membership campaign. This will make it easier to segment them and to help verify the effectiveness of special retention efforts undertaken on their behalf.

- Target these members for a special follow up. Contact them three to six months after joining to ascertain their level of satisfaction.

- Deal with any concerns these new members have on an individual basis, versus in a group.

139

50 Ideas
That Can Help
Retain Members
in the Millennium
Marketplace

29. During functions, suggest that officers look for new members and spend time with them. Make sure new members' name tags indicate their status. New forms of networking include teleconferences, chat rooms, listserves, and other electronic interactions. One advantage membership organizations have over the private sector in the new millennium is the ability to also bring people together in person, to provide the human contact people still need. Some people, however, are not comfortable in large groups, especially if they don't know anyone else there. New members often fall into this category. If a member attends only one meeting and is uncomfortable, that is the membership experience on which he or she might base the decision to renew.

To put new members at ease and make the networking experience a positive one, make sure staff and volunteers can easily identify people attending their first function. This is usually done by having new members wear a special name tag or ribbon. Some groups don't want to make new members feel more conspicuous, so they use a less obvious means of identification.

Whatever method is used, the key to making new members feel welcome is the behavior of other members, not the type of name tag. Volunteer leaders should have the responsibility of seeking out new members and spending time with them at organizational functions. In many organizations the top volunteers are also leaders in the industry, profession, or community and are among the people the new members would most like to meet. New members who are acknowledged by leaders gain recognition within the organization, and the current members feel part of the organization's membership retention efforts.

30. Scan industry, professional, and community publications, as well as the Internet, for ads by members. Look through newspapers, magazines, and other business or professional publications to identify current members who are advertisers. Whenever you spot a member's ad that does not carry your organization's logo or some sign of affiliation, contact the member and remind him or her that this affiliation can be a competitive advantage. Encourage the member to use the organization's logo on future ads. Once the member gets used to using the logo they won't want to drop out and lose that valuable marketing tool. *(Note: To avoid any appearance of endorsing a particular member or product, consult your legal counsel and establish policies for proper use of the organization's logo.)*

One value of membership is the ability to use the organization as a vehicle for marketing products or services. Members who feel connected to the organization are more likely to continue their memberships. So using the affiliation with a membership organization as a part of a marketing effort means that everyone wins—the organization gets an involved member, and the member gets value from the organizational affiliation.

31. Give members points when they participate in any activity. Whenever members buy publications, attend meetings, and so on, award activity points that can be exchanged for various incentives. Like the frequent flyer programs sponsored by the airlines, such an incentive program can encourage members to participate in more activities. Points could be awarded for sponsoring a new member, purchasing publications or other materials, enrolling in an organization-sponsored benefit program, responding to a member survey (via phone, fax, e-mail, or mail), participating in a distance-learning activity such as an online seminar or telephone program, or writing an article for a publication.

Incentives earned through this type of program might include reduced dues for the next year, discounted or free publications or educational programs, preferred seating at organizational functions, or special listings in organizational publications.

Although this program may require additional time and effort to develop, once underway, it could attract enough interest to create a friendly competition among members. Ideally, it will remind members who have not been active that there is still a reward for minimal levels of participation.

32. Send an audiocassette, compact disk (CD), or floppy disk to members as an informal annual report. Few people take the time to read all of the material contained in annual reports produced by companies and membership organizations, so they may be unaware of all the good work an organization has done on their behalf during the past year. In lieu of—or in addition to—a printed annual report, highlight your organization's accomplishments in other formats. An annual report on audiotape or CD—featuring the narration of a volunteer leader—allows the member to listen while driving in a car or sitting in an office. Plus, you can present information more informally, in a conversational tone, with the

141

50 Ideas
That Can Help
Retain Members
in the Millennium
Marketplace

narrator using voice inflection and volume to make points and hold listeners' attention.

For members who prefer using computers to review information, make the annual report available on floppy disk, CD-ROM, or as a download item from your Web site.

33. Establish a Member Service Center for "one-stop shopping." Customers and members may feel more comfortable dealing with your organization if they can go to a central place for assistance. A member service center is the first line of contact between the organization and the member. Instead of phone calls starting with a receptionist or general phone answering service menu, they are forwarded to a centralized area where customer service center personnel are trained to handle frequently asked questions; there is no need to transfer the caller to several staff people before he or she gets an answer.

The Member Service Center has worked well for many groups, including the Instrument Society of America (ISA International), Research Triangle Park, N.C. ISA's system allows specially trained member service representatives to handle routine calls from members quickly and efficiently. At the same time, these staffers can update member records to reflect the activity of that particular transaction; "cross-sell" other ISA products, services, and functions; and try to convert nonmember callers into members.

By tracking member activity via this centralized member service center, ISA is able to send customized membership renewal notices.

34. Offer money-back guarantees on all programs and services (including membership). In almost every interaction, the member compares your organization to private companies and other service providers. One customer service technique that has contributed to the success of some firms is offering a money-back guarantee: If not satisfied with a product or service for any reason, the customer can have his or her money refunded. Many firms offering this incentive also have a "no questions asked" policy, meaning the customer doesn't have to explain or defend the decision to request a refund. The company would like to know the source of dissatisfaction but doesn't put pressure on the customer to be specific.

Membership organizations should adopt the same policy. If a member purchases a publication and is disappointed enough to ask for his or her money back, the organization should comply. It will lose much more than the cost of the refund if the member is upset enough to tell others about the interaction. The old saying "buyer beware" is fine with a private firm producing a single product, but members have a different attitude toward their membership organizations. How they are treated is important to customers, but they don't have a relationship with a private firm that continues after the transaction occurs. If customers don't like the interaction with a company, they simply sever the relationship and no longer do business with it in the future.

In a membership organization, however, a dissatisfied customer may still have months to go before the current year's membership ends. In that case, the member now feels bound to an organization with which he or she just had a bad experience. During the member's remaining time, the membership experience is likely to deteriorate. Offering a money-back guarantee won't ensure the member's renewal but will create a positive image at renewal time.

Whether to extend the money-back guarantee to membership itself is a more complicated matter. In some organizations, the membership fees are so high that refunding the dues of dissatisfied members could cause financial instability. In organizations where the membership dues are relatively low, however, the money-back guarantee might be an option. It would certainly be the ultimate statement of confidence by the organization to tell members they can get their membership investment back if they aren't happy with their decision to join.

143

50 Ideas
That Can Help
Retain Members
in the Millennium
Marketplace

35. Establish standards for responding to members.
When evaluating membership organizations, members often consider responsiveness—the manner in which inquiries are answered and how quickly the answers arrive. Saying that member retention is directly related to providing good service may seem like an old-fashioned notion, but it remains true even in the new marketplace. In addition, the member (customer) determines good service, not the organization.

To be responsive and provide good service, your organization must establish standards. Examples include setting guidelines for how quickly calls are answered (for example, by the third ring), how quickly calls are returned (for example, within three hours), how quickly staff and leaders are expected to respond to faxes and e-mail messages, etc. The actual standards may vary from one group to the next; standards that seem reasonable for one organization may be beyond the resources of another.

Once established, the standards for response and service should be communicated to all of the people who are responsible for meeting them. Also consider communicating your standards of service to customers and members so they will know what to expect.

36. When conducting focus groups at meetings, invite attendees who are *not* leaders to participate. Through focus groups, members who may never serve in a leadership role can feel their input is still valued. Although members who attend organizational functions are not typically those most likely to drop out, their attendance at meetings is another opportunity to gather information about what values various membership segments are seeking from your organization.

37. Send mini-surveys that can be done quickly (via fax). Members appreciate the shorter time needed to respond to mini-surveys and are glad you asked for their opinion. Organizations that use this technique often register a high response rate, compared to longer, more-involved member interest surveys. A mini-survey is another way to get members—perhaps targeted segments—involved in the organization in a way that is meaningful but not necessarily time consuming.

38. Develop a telephone orientation for new members. In smaller organizations, the new member orientation has been a staple of membership retention efforts for years. As time constraints on new members and volunteer leaders increase, such orientations are becoming impractical. One option is to develop a new member orientation done over the telephone. Call or write ahead so the member can set aside 10 to 15 minutes to ask questions and listen to information. Although not as effective as a face-to-face or a group orientation, it allows you to verify that new members have received certain information and to gather additional demographic information.

145

50 Ideas
That Can Help
Retain Members
in the Millennium
Marketplace

To interest members in telephone orientations, set ground rules before the call. These include a scheduled time for the call, a set length of time (perhaps 10 minutes), questions sent in advance so the member can prepare responses, and adequate preparation for the person doing the orientation. People are too busy to spend 20 or 30 minutes talking about an organization in general terms. If, however, the call has a purpose and is handled in a professional, friendly way, new members are more likely to participate.

39. Consider offering a multi-year membership at a reduced rate. Another way to emulate the private sector is to offer discounted fees or dues for multi-year memberships. This gives your organization additional income to invest, allows the member to save money and avoid the annual renewal process, reduces the time and money spent on the dues-collection process, minimizes paperwork, and gives you an early warning of who the late payers may be.

Offering a multi-year membership requires careful planning, however. To be sure multi-year dues payers aren't lost in the ongoing management of the membership function, consider the following techniques.

- Work with your financial managers to account for the multi-year members and to budget for slightly reduced dues income each year.

- Make sure membership records accurately reflect the new renewal schedule for these members.

- Remind multi-year members of the value of membership. If, for example, you send an annual report to members before renewals go out, send the report to multi-year members, too.

- Instead of sending a renewal notice to multi-year members, send an annual information update form. Point out that they don't owe any money but that your organization wants to be certain its records are up to date to ensure the continuance of good service.

40. Consider offering a multi-employee discount to companies that pay for employees' dues. Most individual membership organizations can identify companies or institutions with more than one employee member. They might be able to gain greater corporate support and better assist their members by establishing a discounted dues program for employers who pay dues for multiple memberships. The more employees who are members, the lower the cost per employee. This technique might encourage the employer to get more employees involved in the organization.

41. Set up a system that allows members to renew electronically. In the new marketplace, electronic interchange of information and e-commerce (buying products and services online) will become the norm. Begin working with your financial institutions and technology professionals to make an electronic renewal service available to members as soon as possible.

42. Consider allowing members to create their own membership package. In virtually every organization there are members who wonder why they need to pay full dues when they use only part of the organization's programs or services. In the new marketplace, members, with more choices than ever before, will take an even harder look at the fact that they are paying for services they don't use. Membership organizations should consider letting members design their own memberships. For example, for a basic, reduced fee members can pick two or three services they want included in their membership, with the understanding that any additional services are available for additional fees.

43. When a new member joins, e-mail congratulations from an organizational leader that same day. Technology allows for immediate follow up and contact, so why wait several days or weeks to welcome new members? As new members join, add their e-mail addresses to the membership database. Wherever possible, the recruiter should contact the headquarters office or the membership coordinator and supply the names and e-mails of the new members. As soon as a member joins—preferably the same day—e-mail a brief message of congratulations.

Doing this shows the new member he or she is valued by the organization; emphasizes that the new member is an individual, not a number; illustrates the organization's ability to respond and follow up quickly; overcomes the break in communication that occurs between the time someone joins and the organization makes its first contact; and alerts the new member to expect receipt of the new member information.

The e-mail message can be as simple as: "Congratulations! I just heard from our organization's membership chair that you (your company) joined our organization today. You just made a great investment in your future (career), and I hope you get as much benefit from your membership as I've received from mine. Your New Member Packet should arrive in a few days.

147

50 Ideas
That Can Help
Retain Members
in the Millennium
Marketplace

Look it over and contact me if you have any questions. Welcome to our organization.—Bill Smith, President.''

The message is short and to the point and doesn't ask the new member for anything. It's just a celebration of the decision to join.

44. Look into posting results of meetings and conferences on the Internet. On the one hand, you don't want to jeopardize attendance at meetings by making the proceedings and educational programs too easily available to those who don't attend. On the other hand, members don't always have the time to attend in person yet may still wish to know the latest information in the field.

Investigate ways to make information available to nonattendees via your Web site. Options include charging for the information, delaying release of the information until a certain period after the meeting or convention ends, or offering summaries rather than the entire text of presentations.

45. Increase meeting attendance by featuring an interview with the meeting's keynote speaker in the publication that comes out a month before the meeting. Meeting attendance has traditionally been a basic measurement of member involvement. To keep this important aspect and benefit of membership viable in the new marketplace, use the credibility of the keynote speaker to attract busy people to the meeting. In addition to further publicizing the meeting, this interview will give potential attendees more background about the speaker and the opportunity to hear about the upcoming program from the speaker in his or her own words.

46. List new members on your Web site. Traditionally, membership organizations have listed new members in their publications to welcome them and to encourage current members to make contact with them. With more members and prospects looking to an organization's Web sites as their first or main method of interaction, it makes sense to use the Web site to welcome new members.

47. Put individual e-mail addresses of key leaders on your Web site. If a person is visiting your organization's Web site, he or she is probably comfortable with exchanging information electronically. To create a feeling of inclusion for these members, give them the capability to communicate directly with key organization leaders electronically. Put a leadership directory with the e-mail addresses of volunteer and staff leaders on your Web site, along with a list of Web site departments and other basic information.

In the past, contact with volunteer leaders was limited to letters, telephone calls, or faxes to the leader's work place. E-mail makes volunteer leaders more accessible without intruding on their privacy; the volunteer can read his or her e-mail whenever it is convenient. The member contacting the leader feels a greater sense of connection by communicating directly with the leader rather than going through the organization or the member's employment setting. Putting staff e-mail addresses on the Web site enhances the member's perception that your organization is an open and friendly resource.

149

50 Ideas
That Can Help
Retain Members
in the Millennium
Marketplace

48. Combine and coordinate all forms of member communication to support membership recruitment and retention efforts. In the new marketplace, the successful organization won't necessarily be the one with the greatest technological capabilities, the one that contacts its members most frequently, or the one that spends the most on membership development. The organization that will have the greatest success will use *all* of its resources in the most efficient manner.

It won't be enough just to keep pace with various technologies unless you use them to better serve your members. It's not about the organization—it's about the member. Effective organizational leadership will be characterized by combining technology, planning, communications, and empathy to better help members succeed in *their* new environment.

49. Have a special listserve and/or Web site for first-year members. Because first-year members need as much extra attention as possible, why not have a special section of your Web site that is designated for first-year members? These usually are the members who have the most questions about what's going on in the organization, but who are sometimes reluctant to ask questions because they don't want to appear uninformed. Give these first-year members a special password to enter their own part of your Web site. This should give them access to answers to questions frequently asked by first-year members. Don't just repeat information sent to all members in other communications; take some key items and repackage them for new members. For example, if you have a convention or meeting coming up, on the Web page dedicated to first-year members you can reference the meeting and add suggestions for those who will be attending for the first time. Explain how registration works, remind them of what to bring, give anecdotal information about what previous attendees have found useful, etc. Make the first-year member feel as though he or she can attend a function, respond to communications, or get involved as easily and as comfortably as a member who has been around for a while.

50. Deliver the new member kit electronically. Almost all organizations have some type of new member kit/packet that they send to new members soon after accepting their applications. This packet typically contains a sample of almost everything the association has. These kits often include a welcome letter, a directory, a publications listing or catalog, a sample of a recent newsletter or magazine, a survey or member profile form, a sign-up sheet for committees, flyers announcing upcoming events, a membership plaque or card, and so forth. All of this is important information that should be put into the hands of members as soon as possible after they join. However, in the new marketplace, is it realistic to believe that new members are going to go through these voluminous packets and read everything? Probably not.

Instead of delivering these packets through the mail, organizations should consider sending as much of this information as possible electronically. New members can receive (in just a few days after joining) almost all of the same information. The packets can be downloaded at the member's convenience in a format the member prefers and can be stored electronically (rather than bundled into a large folder that never sees the light of day after it is set up). Of course, certain items, such as certificates or membership cards, should not be sent this way, although there may be other electronic alternatives organizations can use (e.g., downloadable membership certificates, online membership directories, etc.). This electronic new member packet needs to be an option (perhaps noted on the application) to members and organizations; do not assume that all new members will prefer to get their new member packet electronically.

151
———
50 Ideas
That Can Help
Retain Members
in the Millennium
Marketplace